A Cockney Kangaroo

Tales of an Eastend kid!

Preface:

The world is vast and growing rapidly. Many of us now consider ourselves to be global citizens. So much of the world's population are first generation, born to immigrant parents and this has possibly given us a somewhat distorted view of our roots, our heritage. For example, mine. I am Australian, but that is by choice. By birth I am English, more specifically a Londoner, but again this is too broad a term to explain to you exactly where I come from. More specifically, I am an East Londoner and you would have to believe that is as specific as you can get, but not so. I am an, "Eastender," born and raised.

To be able to truthfully claim this unique title, a person needed to be born in one of the four districts, directly east of the great City of London, E1, E2, E3 & E14, with the "E" designating East. These four boroughs were made up of a mish-mash of people from all over the world. Russian's, Jews, Lascar's, Greek, Chinese etc. Famous, (or should I say infamous), for the, still unsolved, "Whitechapel murders , the gruesome work of one Jack the Ripper in1888. This was a unique place to be, in a unique time in history, that no longer exists today.

I spent the first 25 years of my life in Poplar, E.14, before eventually leaving for the promise of sunshine and oranges, hallway across the world away in Australia.

Chapter 1.

"A Real Cockney Boy?"

Whitechapel,(E1), Bow,(E3), Poplar, (E14), and E2 being Bethnal Green, the birthplace of the Kray twins, whose criminal trial was, (and still is) the longest murder trial in British Criminal History. In 1969 at London's famous Old Bailey Court, the brothers received a sentence of 30 years without parole for the murders of George Cornell in the Blind Beggar Pub and Jack "the hat" Mcvitie in Evering Rd, Stoke Newington.

You see, I am part of an almost extinct & unique group of Londoners, ones who claim a very specific set of circumstances that, when joined together, entitles them to call themselves "Cockneys". But what exactly is a Cockney, and more importantly, what determines whether or not a person can honestly & genuinely call him or herself, "A true Cockney"?

Trying to get a definition of the word Cockney from a dictionary or encyclopaedia will often lead to confusion and if you happen to be anywhere in London, quite possibly an argument and very possibly fisticuffs!

There are many personal and vehemently different views on what a real cockney is. Officially, as well as to many Londoners, it means "a native of East London, traditionally one born within hearing of The Bow Bells", but what does this mean? What are, (and indeed where are) 'The Bow Bells'?
Growing up as a kid in East London, I always thought that "within the sound of Bow Bells," referred to the bells of Bow Church, a church of England house of worship located on an island in the middle of Bow Road, in the East London suburb of Bow E3. The full name for this lovely old church is, "St Mary and Holy Trinity, Stratford, Bow,".
My childhood home in Ellesmere St, Poplar E14 was close enough to this church, (and because I had that "easily recognisable East London accent") I always just assumed, that's it! I'm a Cockney. Of course, as young children who make assumptions often are, I was totally wrong. Not the right church, not even in the right location.

The "Bow Bells" referred to in the definition of a Cockney are in fact, the bells of the church of "St Mary-le-Bow" which can be found in Cheapside, inside the walls of the, "one-mile- square," City of London.
Google maps refers to St Mary-le-Bow Church as, "Church that defines London's Cockneys." So, anyone who claims to

be a Cockney because they were in fact "born within the sound of Bow Bells" must be correct.

But are they?

As I have already said, there has always been and continues to be enormous debate, sometimes even leading to heated arguments about this, especially over the last eighty or so years, since the end of WW2. Why that time frame? Simple: because much of that beautiful old church was destroyed by a German bomb during the Blitz on 10 May 1941. The result on this aerial onslaught caused a massive fire to engulf this historic building, during which the bells crashed to the ground.

The building, rebuilt by Sir Christopher Wren following the Great Fire of London in 1666, was completely destroyed and the twelve great bells that had rung out over London and heard by generations, including the largest of the twelve, "The Big Bell of Bow," mentioned in the nursery rhyme, crashed to the ground, another victim of Hitler's blitz.. So, given the Bells would not ring for twenty or so years, does that mean there were no Cockneys born during that time? It would be two decades before those bells would be re-cast from the original's in the Whitechapel Bell Foundry and re-hung in the newly rebuilt church.

Many people still proclaim that there were no Cockney's born during this hiatus and endeavouring to prove them right or wrong is an onerous, never-ending task.

As for me, well, I was born in the East End Maternity Hospital in Commercial Road, E1, in the middle of a German V1 rocket air raid, in the early hours of July 27, 1944. Even though Hitler and his blitz did their best to stop my arrival, and albeit temporarily silenced the splendid sound of the mighty Bow Bells, I consider myself to be a true Cockney boy, born & bred and I bet I'm not the only one!!!

Very soon after I made my entry into this world, it was time to be evacuated out of the mayhem that was East London at the time. Once the V1 rockets, or "Doodlebugs," as they were called by Londoners, stopped reigning their evil down upon us, Mum walked up the stairs leading from the hospital basement, followed by a midwife carrying a bomb-proof-crib, with me inside. Along with the other mothers & babies, we were loaded into a bus and the driver set off for the safe haven of Newport Pagnell, in Buckinghamshire.

There was no way of knowing or even guessing as to what was in store following my unusual and somewhat perilous beginning. The journey for Mum, myself and our fellow bus travellers, was indeed, a difficult, even dangerous trip. The 75 miles from bomb ravaged East London to the safe haven of Newport Pagnell was completed in total darkness. The, "Blackout," as it was referred to, meant that no lights, of any kind could be used, especially in the city. Hitler's Luftwaffe were still active, and any lights could easily be seen by his bombers, and used as a, "target," releasing even more fear & desolation upon the long suffering people below.

I have no idea as to how the driver of the bus managed to achieve this driving feat, however we arrived at the large stately home of Tyringham Hall, Newport Pagnell, Buckinghamshire just before daybreak. This lovely old building was owned by the widow of a New York banker, Frederick Adolphus Konig, who upon her husband's passing, made the home available for expectant mothers from the East London Maternity Hospital. Many "War babies," were actually born there in Newport Pagnell from 1940 on, when the Hospital was used to treat casualties of the blitz.

It is strangely ironic, that at the same time as the Nazi War Machine was destroying the great cities of England and attempting to eliminate as many of her subjects as was possible, many tiny little "Cockney Babies," were being sheltered, away from all this mayhem, in a beautiful stately home, owned at the time by none other than, a German Baroness, widow, Gertrude Koning, (nee von Chappius), born in Saxony, Germany and one time Lady-in-Waiting to Princess Marie-Louise, granddaughter of Queen Victoria.

On behalf of all of those kids, including myself, "THANKYOU!"

After close to five years of living in war torn Britain, Mum longed to return to London and despite the dangers, she went back to Ellesmere Street in September of that same year. Aged thirty four at the time, a survivor of the first world war, mother of two sons, (my brother Bob, born in 1941), and me. Despite the bombings, the devastation & the dangers she felt safer in the east end.

Within months, the danger became too great and once again we were all evacuated once more, this time to Rochdale, in the great County of Lancashire.

The V1 rockets, or doodlebugs and buzz bombs as they were known were really just a, "flying bomb." Launched from various sites along the French and Dutch coasts, they had limited range, and minimal guidance system. They simply flew, like an unmanned aeroplane, until such time that they ran out of fuel. The noise made by the "Pulsejet," that propelled them was horrific, and designed to scare the good people of England. It was the first time in history that, "Terror Bombing," was utilised.

The maximum speed of a V1 was 640 kmh, flying quite low at less than 900 metres. The British RAF aeroplanes were considerably slower. Even at maximum speed they could not match the speed, however they would fly their "Spitfires or Hurricanes," in the same direction as the rocket, and as they came level, the pilot would, "flip the wing," which in turn would flip the wing of the V1, causing it to stall and drop, hopefully over farmland, where it would do minimal damage. Despite the great work of these flying heroes, most got through to London and when their fuel was exhausted, the flame from the jet would disappear, as would the droning sound. This was the time Londoners grew very anxious. The V1 would not simply drop or fall out of the sky, instead it would glide, like an ominous bird hanging in the sky by its wings.

On one such occasion, my father was on the Isle of Dogs, standing on top of a large tank that contained diesel fuel. He had a long pole in his hand that he used as a, "dipstick," to determine the amount of fuel stored there. He watched as a doodlebug flew down towards him, slowly and silently carving a large circle in the sky. As it flew above him, it seemed to be low enough for him to reach up and touch, however he freely admitted he was far too frightened to dare attempt such a thing, (it was also most likely far too high to do this). He watched it glide across the River Thames, then disappear into South London.

If the infamous and awful V1 was to terrorise and torment the good people of London, the V2 was far worse.

Hitler's, 'vengeance' rocket as it was known, was unleased upon England in the autumn of 1944, (about the same time Mum returned to Poplar from Newport Pagnell). 1,400 V2's were launched from Europe, all aimed at England. They had a range of 320 km's, a speed of 5,700 km's/hour. They weighed 12.5 tonnes, with a warhead weighing close to 1,000kg's and stood 14 meters high. They were in fact, the first use of ballistic missiles in history and more that 500 fell on London, killing no less than 2,754 souls, with a further 6,500 injured.

To escape this madness, unleashed by the Nazi War machine, poor old Mum was to move yet again, this time to the industrial heart of the North, Rochdale.

Situated approximately 10 km's north of Manchester, in the great County of Lancashire, Rochdale was a booming town before the war. Dotted by huge buildings, where thousands of locals found work running the huge & noisy machines that produced textiles. One of those workers was to become Mum's host, when she was evacuated, with my brother & I in late 1944.

Mr Taylor was partially deaf as a result of years in the Clover Mill, where he had worked since leaving school at the age of fifteen. Together with his wife, they lived in a small terraced house at 81 Clarke Street. Their children had grown and left before the war, so the back bedroom, (one of only two), became home for the three of us. Dad stayed in London, but would visit whenever he drove his lorry north.

Mr & Mrs Taylor were wonderful people, sharing what little they had with us, until it was safe to return to the Capital at the end of the war.

We returned for a holiday with the Taylor's in 1949, as they had become good friends. I remember taking Mr Taylor's lunch to his workplace, The Clover Mill and the noise of the machines was deafening. They were a testament to the Industrial revolution of the late 1800's and early 1900's that transformed that part of the north of England. Sadly it was to disappear after the war.

Thousands of families were evacuated from London and the kindness & generosity of people, like the Taylor's was amazing.

A belated special, "Thank you," to all of them!

Having survived all of this, I was about to be raised and to grow up in a unique and special place, London! Not the place that the Romans built, (then called Londinium), and not the place that was rebuilt after the Great Fire of London, but a city that had been un-mercilessly bombed and devastated by fire and suffered a huge death toll. Bombed factories, warehouses, shops and homes were everywhere and were to become the playgrounds for thousands of kids, me included. This would be the world that I would grow up in, go to school in, start work in etc, until………………………………………………………

On a very warm night in August, 1970, the 10th day of August to be exact, just two weeks after my 26th birthday, my Irish-born wife & I made our way from Bellingham in South London, to Gatwick Airport. It was dark as we walked behind a large group of people, crossing the tarmac, heading towards a, "Caledonian Airways," aircraft. Immediately in front of us was a family of five, with all of their hand luggage, and three very tired kids, they were struggling a little. Joan, my wife being the kind compassionate nurse she is, stepped in and helped, taking the hand of the youngest child. This family had left Birmingham 15 hours earlier, so they were very grateful for the support.
As we approached the aircraft, we were told to use the rear door. With Joan and the Birmingham family in front of me, I

put one foot on the bottom step, then my other foot stepped off of England, the only home I had ever known.

At that point in time, I was another "£10 POM," as indeed were all of the people on that Qantas Charter Flight, and like the many thousands of migrants who had made this journey before us, we were bound for Sydney, Australia. All of us had completed all of our interviews with the staff at Australia House in London, paid our £10 and with a head full of dreams, said our goodbyes to family and friends, and boarded the flight that would change our lives forever.

More of that Kangaroo story later. In the meantime, back to my days as a Cockney!

Chapter 2.

Oranges and Lemons!

In September of 1945, the second world war finally came to an end. For the good people of London, it was not soon enough. In Poplar, everybody celebrated, danced in the streets and did whatever they could to rejoice the fact that they had come through six dark and terrible years, and much to their surprise but utmost delight, they had survived. The courage, strength and resilience of those who went through it is legendary. I am in total awe of all of them and cannot begin to imagine how they got through!

One of my first childhood memories are those of the summer of 1951. Just five short years after the war finished, Britain celebrated with, "The Festival of Britain." I can vaguely remember walking up Chrisp Street, crossing East India Dock Rd and waiting outside the great structure of All Saints Church. The Luftwaffe had managed to hit this beautiful building many times, and a V2 rocket destroyed the roof in 1945. I watched the repair work in progress, as Dad & I stood waiting for our tram ride into the City. Post-War London was an absolute wonderland for me as a child and a trip into it with my Father was the best treat ever. Passing by some of the old landmarks, such as the Aldgate Pump, The Mansion House, Bank of England, (which my Father explained was known as, "The Old Lady of Threadneedle Street), the amazing Sir Christopher Wren built St Pauls Cathedral, all still standing, (although many were damaged), despite the war. Under Blackfriars Arch, up Ludgate Hill, Fleet Street, the Strand, Charing Cross and Trafalgar Square. We walked down Whitehall, past the Horse guards' parade, Downing Street, the Cenotaph until we came upon the world famous, "Big Ben."

I held on tight to my Dad's hand, as we crossed Westminster bridge then onto the Southbank to see the exhibition. I can clearly remember the huge Dome of Discovery, which showed all the plans for rebuilding England, and the 300 foot high Skylon, which was illuminated every night, to show that the future was bright for our country.

Poplar was also included in the Festival and in fact played a major role in celebrating the half-century. The bombing had left huge areas of E14 desolate, and many people homeless, so construction began on the Lansbury Estate, named after George Lansbury, a Poplar councillor and Labour MP, (and Grandfather to Mary Poppins herself, the great English actress, Angela Lansbury). It included Chrisp Street market, Susan Lawrence School, as well as a mixture of housing types, all of which still stand today, some seventy years later.

Ellesmere Street today, runs from Upper North Street to Alton Street, but in 1951 it continued on, crossed Godalming Road and finished at Chrisp Street. Number 46 was on the south side of the street. There were two other houses and a corner bombed site, before crossing Chrisp Street, where you would be met by the eerie sight of the bombed ruin of St Gabriel's Church. Mum & Dad were married there in 1938, but in 1951 it consisted of two large walls, coming to a point at the top, and timbers that had once supported the slate tile roof, stretched between the walls, leaving only the skeleton of what once was!

There was approximately 12 kids living in Ellesmere Street in 1951, and that included only that part of the street between Chrisp St and Godalming Road. All of us war babies, coming from poor families, living in houses that were propped up with huge timbers to stop them falling down. Most of us wearing second-hand clothes, worn out shoes, basically anything that could be found after the war. Nobody locked their doors, and everybody helped each other.

It is interesting to me, that history refers to these times & locations, using terms such as, "tough times," and "extreme hardship," etc. etc. The irony of this is that I never heard anyone says these, or any similar things when I was a kid. To us Cockney's, that was life! It was the way we lived, and it was all we knew. At that age I just assumed that the whole world was like this, after all, my whole word was. Didn't everyone live in a little house like mine? Didn't everyone play on the debris? I do not deny that history is correct. I simply say, that I believe the vast majority of us East Londoner's, just did not acknowledge it.

Me, aged 5 in my brothers Cub Uniform in the backyard of number 46 in 1949.

Our playground, as little kids was the street, (no cars around then), and the bomb sites, or the, "Debris'," as we called them. One of the favourite games for the girls, (and boys sometimes), was skipping. Someone would have a long piece of rope, most probably unknowingly donated by one of the ships chandlers in the nearby docks and with a "turner" on each end, you could jump in, and skip or as the Americans would say, "jump rope." To keep time, many songs were sung, some new, and others passed down by previous generations. The one I remember most, is one that just about every Londoner would have heard, but I am certain every single Cockney would have sung as a kid, and remembered all of their life?

Oranges & Lemons!

Oranges and Lemons,
Say the Bells of St Clement's.

You owe me five farthings,
Say the Bells of St Martin's.

When will you pay me?
Say the bells at Old Bailey

When I grow rich,

Say the bells at Shoreditch.

When will that be?
Say the bells of Stepney.

I do not know,
Says the big bell at **Bow.**

As the big piece of rope turned across the street, from kerb to kerb, and the girls sung the song, we would take turns to run in, and sing and skip to this very old, and beautiful song. The churches in the song are most likely:

St Clement's is St Clement Danes which is close to the wharves where citrus fruits were once landed (thus Oranges & Lemons).

St Martin's may be St Martin Ongar in the city, or St Martin-in-the-Fields, near Trafalgar Square.

St Sepulchre-without-Newgate, opposite the the **Old Bailey**.

St Leonard's **Shoreditch**, just outside the City walls.

St Dunstan's **Stepney** Green, also outside the city.

The big bell of **Bow** is the largest of the twelve bells at Saint Mary-le-Bow in Cheapside, in the City.

Saint Mary-le-Bow church is only one mile from the east gate of the old City of London, Aldgate, so the sound of this massive bell would have been easily heard by those people who lived and worked in the hamlets that existed along the north bank of the Thames, one of which is called Tower Hamlets, (which includes Poplar) today.

Chapter 3.

"More 'ot' in number 6 please!"

Our little house, at number 46 Ellesmere Street Poplar, was one, of a line of terraced houses, built in 1864, and named, "Arthur Cottages."
When they were first constructed, they formed a line of identical dwellings, that stretched from Chrisp Street to Godalming Road, however I never saw all of those buildings. The building on the corner of Chrisp Street had been for many years a general shop, but by the time I arrived into the world, Hitler had managed to destroy this, plus the two houses next door, leaving a vacant lot in their place. The very same thing had occurred at the other end, with four buildings blown to bits, and another vacant block, on which a brick & concrete bomb shelter had been built.

As a result, there remained only six of the original buildings, and to keep them from falling over, large timber frames were erected, one on number 40 on the western end and one on number 50. In addition there were two lengths of steel rod, placed all the way through the attics of the six houses, and secured in place with very large saucer shaped steel plates, and nuts, tightened up to hold our homes together, like a giant Meccano set.

Once inside there was a narrow passage, with the back door at the far end. Two rooms to the right, front room and living room, separated by eleven narrow stairs, leading up to two bedrooms, Mum & Dads at the front and us kids in the back.

Behind the Living Room was a small room which we called, "the scullery." It contained a gas cooker/oven, and a large sink. Attached to the back of that was our outside toilet, complete with a wooden seat, a piece of rope with which to flush, and a piece of wire on the wall on which to hang the toilet paper, usually the Daily Mirror or the Radio Times, as toilet paper was a luxury we couldn't buy, (or afford) in those days.

No bath, no shower, in fact no hot water, so every second Friday the tin bath was taken down from the nail that held it in place on the outside back wall, and the kettle and saucepans were put on the stove in the scullery and the bath placed on the floor in front of the fire. The hot water was carried in, and when ready, into the bath us kids would go, eldest first, then the younger ones. I only had one brother older than me, so the water was literally second hand, however, some houses had as many as 10 kids, so being last in their house meant lukewarm water, with the strong smell of Lifebuoy Soap, and a very strange looking film floating on the top. The thing was, we did not know that we were poor, and this was in no way different to how the rest of the world cleaned themselves, so we loved our bath night, (or at least I did).

Once we reached an age where we were big enough, the old tin bath was no longer used, at least not to bathe in. Filled with soil, (or dirt as we called it), usually taken from one of the bombed sites after dark, the redundant tub was placed in the small backyard, and for many years thereafter, it supplied us with veggie's, or flowers. Nothing was wasted in the east end in those days.
It never fails to amaze me and puts a wry smile on my face, when I hear parents today, telling their kids they must shower every day!!! Of course I understand the need to keep clean, and showers are now the chosen way to go, but when I think back to the 50's, in Poplar, things were a bit different. Once we were too big for the old tin bath, and we could walk up Chrisp Street on our own, it was time for one of life's great pleasures, Poplar Baths. My Dad used to insist we keep clean too, so he would tell us, "you go for a bath every second Friday, whether you need it or not!"

In a war ravaged East London, with its huge areas of destruction, Polar baths stood out like a beacon. On East

India Dock Rd, right opposite the top end of Chrisp Street market, it was an architect's delight. The original had been built under the, "Baths and Washhouses Act,"
of 1846, rebuilt in 1933, bombed during the Second World War and reopened in 1947.
Inside was a large swimming pool, which could be covered, (and was during the cold winters), and regularly staged boxing and wrestling events. I remember going there with my Dad to see a, "Freestyle Wrestling Match," in the late 1950's, however I digress.

Walking into the building, the nose was hit with the strong smell of chlorine. In front was the ticket office and depending on your status, (or should I say, how much money you had), you could choose, a, "First Class or Second Class bath." As I write this today, in my mid-70's, I must confess, I never saw what the First Class bath looked like. Second class was our choice, easily made because Mum would give us exactly ninepence. For this we would pay sixpence for the bath, a penny for the towel, another for a bath cube, (without which the soap would not lather in the hard London water), and a penny to be spent at the Café when the ablutions were complete.

Ticket, towel and cube in hand, it was upstairs to the, "Men's Second Class Baths," and wait for the attendant. Within a short time he would appear, dressed in white trousers and a white singlet. His name, (or at least what everybody called him), was Jock. He had a strong Scottish accent, and huge horn-rimmed glasses. "Follow me," he would say, and we would walk through a narrow corridor, which consisted of wooden partitions on both sides, with doors every six feet or so. Every door had a number, and next to each door , at waist height was a large square chrome plate, with a hole in the middle.

Going through into, "your cubicle," you were met with a very large, (or so it looked at my age then), bathtub. A wooden stool for you to sit upon whilst getting undressed, and a hook on the wall for your clothes and towel.

Once the door was closed, Jock would go outside, and using is "Special Key," he would turn the water on, and the huge tap would gurgle, and spurt water into the tub. Throw in the bath cube, quickly get undressed, (especially in the winter) and climb into your very own, nobody else has used, clean, hot water……bliss!

After a short soak, it was time for a top-up. Moving to the far end of the tub away from that massive tap, it's your turn to join the chorus, that you had been listening to, whilst soaking. The call was the same, but with one unique difference, that being the number of the cubicle that you were in. Taking a deep breath, and using all the voice you could muster, you yell……….

More "ot" in number 6 please!

Jock would duly arrive and the sound of his Special Key would be heard, going into the hole in the chrome plate on the other side of the partition, then that Scottish lament was heard, "mind your feet," and the tap would supply a burst of hot water, which you would immediately swirl around, before it would stop, and Jock would be gone. A second short soak to enjoy this lovely warm water was in order, however, if you soaked to long, those dulcet scots tones would be heard again, complemented with a loud bang on the door, "times up number 6," which meant you immediately vacated the tub, quickly dried and dressed, left the towel on the wooden stool, then went off to spend that last penny.

The little café in Poplar baths was magical to me. They sold all sorts of snacks, and sweets, but for me the, "Doorstep-Toast," was just the best thing ever! Almost an inch thick, toasted to a dark brown, and covered in butter, (real butter, still a luxury for us in those days), and handed over in a piece of grease-proof-paper, in exchange for that penny. Walking home past the stalls in Chrisp Street, squeaky clean, with a slice of the best treat ever, was the way we kept clean, and I still cherish those early memories. They were very much a part of my early Cockney upbringing.

Chapter4.

Lower the Drawbridge.

Growing up in Poplar in the Eastend in the early 1950's was an amazing experience. I have outlined several reasons for this already and I have a lot more in my repertoire that I will reference. So many stories, tales and anecdotes of a childhood lived in a time with very few material possessions. You see, we did not have all the fancy stuff that the kids of today enjoy. Don't get me wrong, I have no envy or jealousy. Actually, I think its brilliant that things such as X-Box, Nintendo etc. are around today. Activities such as watching movies on a Tablet and talking to friends via video call on a Smartphone is what today's young people are all about. I do however have one small observation to make and one simple question to put to you: do the kids of today have, or can they develop the same type of imagination that we had?

All the modern day devices that kids now have access to, pretty much do everything for them. Full colour digitised screens, "in-your-face" graphics and 24/7 access to anything and everything gives this generation, nothing to think about! Games and pastimes with zero imagination required. If they don't know something? GOOGLE it!

Us post-war Cockney kids had none of this stuff, but we still had lots of great times. Roy Rogers, Tom Mix, Gene Autry and Hop-along Cassidy were some of our heroes and we could become any one of them any time that we wanted. France had given us the Three Musketeers to emulate, but my all-time favourite game was when we re-enacted the greatest Englishman of them all, Robin Hood. All it took was a little imagination.

Now I'm certain you have all heard the story of Robin Hood, who stole from the rich to give to the poor and lived with his band of merry men in Sherwood Forest! His sworn enemy was the evil Sherriff of Nottingham. The unfair and unjust taxes he imposed on the good people of Nottinghamshire were causing severe hardship, so Robin set about retrieving as much as he could from the Sherriff's stronghold of Nottingham Castle, and returning it to the poor. Perhaps growing up poor gave us a better understanding of the story, or maybe every kid in England felt that way in the 50's! Who knows, either way, we loved to make believe that we, the brave merry men of Sherwood Forrest could defeat the evil Sheriff and help the poor and of course, the good guys would always win!

One of the largest bombed sites in our Eastend was on the corner of Morris Rd & Rifle Street and was used regularly by all the local kids. Rifle Street was a dead-end road, with the gates of the, "Far Famed Cake Company," at the bottom end. The open space of the bombed site was on one side of the road and directly opposite that was the premises of a local cartage company by the name of Henry Green & Co. Ltd. There was little traffic in those days and other than the few lorries that belonged to Green's, and an occasional flower or cake delivery truck, Rifle Street was an ideal place for playing all sorts of games.

We had a variety of different games that took turns being in favour at any particular time. These included Cricket, (as long as we could get an old egg box from Flay's the grocers as a wicket!), hopscotch for the girls and of course football for the boys. When we tired of these more structured games we would turn to our imaginations and the bombed site would become any amount of different locations, settings or scenes. These included The wild west, if it was cowboys and Indians, a jousting run for knights & ladies and the planet Mars for "Lost-in Space". For Robin Hood, it became Sherwood Forest and the great Castle of Nottingham.

I remember one particular occasion when we were re-enacting the attack on the castle by Robin and his men. It was an ordinary day and we were playing just as we had dozens of times, when suddenly, things went horribly wrong!

Henry Green had several lorries (that's trucks for anyone who isn't English) in his yard in those days, but, being so close to the end of the war, he still maintained quite a few horses & carts as part of his fleet. It was amazing to see just a single horse, (usually a Shire horse), pulling a huge cart, the tray of which was loaded with all kinds of tools and materials required to rebuild this great but war-torn city. The driver, who always seemed to be a huge mountain of a man to us kids, would have the reins in his hands and the whip in its scabbard beside him. He would sit on the front of the cart, high up on his seat, so as to maintain his view over his horse as the powerful animal pulled away, straining on the shafts. Together with the noise made by the large wooden spoked steel rimmed wheels, clanging and banging on the old cobbled street, it made a picture in history, now sadly forever gone.

It was common practice at the end of the working day for the carts to be place on our bombed site. The driver would put a 'chock' or large wooden wedge under each wheel, lift the massive oak & steel shafts up and over until they slammed back against the cart. This resulted in each of the two shafts pointing skywards, nestled firmly either side of the now empty driver seat.

Now this same bomb site was transformed, simply by using our imaginations into the scene required for our great adventure, featuring all the good (and bad!) people of medieval Nottingham. The ground leading up to the parked cart was now the evil sheriff's Castle forecourt. The tray on the huge cart transfigured into the battlements and lastly, the high driver's seat would become the castle walls with the shafts serving as the drawbridge traversing the imaginary moat to the Castle. It was magic. All of us kids formed ourselves into the two respective groups, those being the Sherriff's Soldiers and Robin's Merry Men and the adventures would begin!

Whilst the game of Robin Hood was played out many times on the bombed site, usually with nothing but loads of fun for all of us kid's, on one day in the summer of 1952 the outcome was far different. My brother, Bob, did not usually join in when we played this particular game, claiming that at the age of 10, he was, "well past all that nonsense," however on this particular occasion he was playing the lead role of Robin himself. Another one of the older boys from Morris Rd, called Ronnie was the Sherriff of Nottingham and while the fight to gain entry to the Castle kept all of us kids busy, Robin & The Sherriff were in a sword fighting duel to the death, in front of the Castle gates. With the noise of a whole bunch of scruffy urchins, screaming and yelling, their wooden swords clacking together, and their voices raised to fever pitch, everyone was having the time of their lives.

With all of this happening around us, Robin's men had fought their way to the battlements, scaled the Castle walls and without hesitation, the order was given, "lower the drawbridge!" With all the strength they could muster, pushing hard on each of those solid oak uprights, the drawbridge (the two very large and heavy shafts of the cart) moved slowly forward and past the fully upright position. With a resounding victory cry and screams of excitement from the merry men, the shafts picked up speed and travelled downwards. Just before they reached the horizontal point, Robin, sword in hand and still in mortal combat with the Sherriff, did not hear when the order was given. Neither did he hear the creaking of the timber as the shafts fell, striking him a massive blow to the top of his head.

In an instant everything was quiet. Nobody moved, we were all simply staring at my brother, who was now lying unconscious on the ground. In a gruesome instance of reality imitating the fantasy of the fight, there he was, not imagined but factually wounded, real blood pouring from the wound on his head.

Once the initial shock passed and reality started to hit home for us, we ran to see if he was alright, all the while wondering if we had perhaps killed him? By the time I got to him he had begun to come around, and slowly sat up, looking blankly at all of us which naturally brought great relief to everyone present. Once he realised what had happened to him he began to curse and abuse Robin Hood's, (forgetting they were **his**) merry men for trying to kill him by "lowering the drawbridge," straight onto his head! All the while the blood continued to pour down his face and neck.

There were no mobile phones in those days with which to call an ambulance. We were a bunch of rough and ready street kids and accidents, from cuts and bruises to broken limbs were not uncommon. They were certainly no reason to panic. The Sherriff, (i.e. Ronnie), produced a towel from somewhere which was wrapped around Bob's head to slow the bleeding and the three of us walked into Morris Rd, turned left and up Chrisp Street, over the Willis Street bridge toward St Leonards Rd, turn right towards Blackwall Tunnel and into Poplar Hospital Casualty Department, a distance of approximately 2.5 km's. After a couple of hours, fourteen stitches to hold his wound together and a nice white bandage wrapped around his head, we traced our footsteps back toward Ellesmere Street, arriving home to the shock , surprise and dismay of our poor Mother.

No X-rays, no CT scans, MRI's or any such like procedures. All of these modern science tools would be available for future generations, but for us, "50's kids," a few stitches was good enough.

They built kids tough in Poplar in those days!!!

Chapter 5.

Horse's Carts & Barges.

Poplar today has very little if any resemblance to the place I knew as a child. The massive tower blocks of Canary Wharf, Canada Square, Harbour Exchange, etc. etc, not to mention the four and five star hotels, The Hilton, Radisson, Novotel, to name just a few, abound in this high-rise metropolis, that we knew simply as, "The Isle of Dogs."
To us kids, who lived and played in this same area, such names were unheard of. Not known to the sons and daughters of the East India, West India and Millwall dock workers. Canary wharf was where the ships came in from the Canary Islands, and unloaded banana's, most of which would end up on the dining

tables in those fine hotels in the Westend. The Eastend, "might," see some on the stalls in Chrisp Street Market, (if we were lucky that is)!

Where generations of Dockers, Lightermen and Stevedores plied their various labours, now thousands of different people work in the offices that dominate the skyline. Global Corporations have taken up residence there, which would have been unimaginable in the post war era. One of the more famous one's being Thomson Reuter. I wonder if any of the people who work there every day are aware that a famous east end family also worked in that very same place?

The statue of Richard Green can be seen, sitting in his chair, looking across East India Dock Rd, at the Lansbury Market. George Green school, named after his father, is adjacent, and both pay tribute to this important family. For more than 100 years, the Green's built and owned ships from their shipyard at Blackwall Point. Whaling ships were built and launched from there, as well as ships that sailed to Australia to bring back gold, mined during the great gold rush of 1851. The site of that shipyard is now occupied by Thomson Reuters.

As kids, despite regularly walking past the statue of Richard Green, and seeing other kids going to the George Green School, we really had little or no interest in such things. Although very much a part of the wonderful and colourful history of East London, to us they were just a part of, "our manner!" Blackwall Point however, held a very different interest altogether.

Our little house in Ellesmere Street held many wonderful memories for me. We would sit in our little kitchen after dinner and listen to the radio. "The Archers," "Lost in Space," were just a few of those we would hear on the BBC Light Programme. There was two chairs, one either side of the fireplace, Mums on the right and Dad's the other side, so Bob & I would sit on the hearth, back to the side of the fireplace, but our heads would be wherever the radio shows took us, whilst being kept toasty warm by the adjacent coal fire.

Charlie the Coalman was a very important person in those days. Every year, starting in mid-summertime, Charlie's horse and cart, loaded up with huge black sacks, would appear on the streets, bringing the fuel needed to keep all of those homes warm during the coming winter. As the big Shire Horse pulled that heavy load of coal into our street, Dad would grab the hand-shovel and bucket, give it to one of us kids, and we knew what we were expected to do! Following Charlie, (and the horse), it would only be a matter of time until that big animal gave us what was an essential additive for our garden. Once this had occurred, and the cart had passed over the "fertiliser," it was a race between all the local kids to see who would get there first and claim this prize for their own.

Charlie would continue on, stopping to supply coals to every household that required it. His black sacks of coal weighed in at , "1 Hundredweight, " (94 kilo's in today's terms) and he would pull each bag onto his back, and walk to wherever the house coal bunker was located, often through the house itself, and into the back garden. Charlie would deliver all 40 bags, before his cart was empty and he would then follow the same daily ritual befitting a man who had loaded, unloaded and delivered no less that 2 Tons of coal.

Us kids knew Charlie's daily agenda very well. Why? Because it meant we could earn a few pennies.

Outside of the Guilford Arms, on the corner of Chrisp St and Godalming Rd was where we would find Charlie's horse & cart. The old horse would have been given a well-earned drink of water, and his nose would be buried inside a nosebag, loaded with hay & oats. Charlie would be in the Public Bar, his nose buried in a pint of Carrington's finest ale. After a few pints, Charlie would return to the cart, remove the nosebag, climb into the driver's seat and say just one word, "Giddup." With one or two of us kids on the back of the cart ,the horse would start the journey home. Charlie would pull his old cap down over his eyes and fall instantly to sleep, leaving the horse to navigate the streets back to the stables at Blackwall Point.

Miraculously, Charlie would wake up just as the gates of, "Coe & Co Ltd, Coal Merchants," appeared. Once inside, he would remove all the leather tack from the horse, and at that point us kids would move in to earn our pay. One of us would lead the horse, (all 17 hands, 900 kilograms of him), into the stable, give him his water, and feed, and shut the stable door. The next job was to clean all the tack and hang it up, then, "muck-out," the stable the horse had slept on the previous night, and leave it clean and with fresh straw, ready for his return on the following day. If we did this well, and depending on how many pints Charlie had consumed, we would be rewarded with a penny, or two for our labours.

This was not the only encounter us kids would have with these big lumbering, but lovable horses.

In the 1700's in response to the pressing need for an alternative to roads, to deliver goods across the UK, various companies built canals. With names denoting the area's they covered, Oxford, Grand Union, Coventry, Trent & Mersey, etc were dug by hand, on average no more than four to five feet in depth, with, "Locks," to control the depth and to rise & fall over the natural contours of the land, bridges spanning over the canals and aqueduct's to carry the canals over roads etc. They were a marvel of modern engineering in their day and are still used today for recreational purposes.

Flat-bottom-barges were constructed, each capable of carrying up to 30 tons and able to be pulled by one Shire Horse. A horse & wagon could only carry 3 ton, so the barges were a significant improvement.

For us Eastend kids, the canals were a big part of our lives. They were a source of adventure, fun, learning new skills plus an opportunity to earn some money. In their heyday, including navigable rivers, there was upwards of 4,000 miles of navigable waterways, but for us kids, the Regents Canal was the best. It was where every local kid would, "go fishing," for their first experience. (See chapter 13 for my own experiences).

Heading down to the canal in the summer holidays was a regular event for me and my mates. There were locks all along the canals and Lock number 8 was in Old Ford, next to Victoria park. Many of the barges were motorised by the late 50's, however there were still many horse-drawn, which presented opportunities to make some money.

We would hang around the locks until one of the horse-drawn barges arrived, then we would ask, "the bargee," if we could help him get through the lock, while he took a tea break. Once we got his permission, we would go into action. One of us would un-hitch the horse from his harness, take him to the water trough for a drink, then give him a feed of oats. Once this was done, we would work together to get the barge into the lock, close the gates and using the bargee's windlass, open the paddles on the lock to let the water flow.

The next step in the process was to pull the barge out of the lock, moor it to the bank, then put the horse back into harness, ready for the bargee to continue his journey, after he gave us a couple of pennies. As he walked off, leading his horse along the towpath, we would head off to the nearest sweetshop for Tizer and ice cream.

I can only wonder what reaction we would get, if we tried to implement this kind of thing with kids today???????

The mind boggles!!!

Chapter 6.

Smells & Slaps.

The diversity of people, nationalities, religions etc in the East-End in the Fifties was amazing. Some evidence of this still exists today, including Jewish beigel shops and Chinese restaurants. Pennyfields is the small street that was known simply as, "Chinatown." It was a place that had all kinds of stories attached to it, most of them very scary to us kids. I distinctly remember being told by both Mum & Dad that we must never go there, especially after dark, and the stories and yarns attached to these warnings pushed the point home.

"They catch, cook and eat Dogs," was one such tale that I remember well. "They will eat you if they catch you," was another which I never really believed, but it certainly instilled fear in us kids, HOWEVER not enough to stop us exploring this mystical and very different place.

Pennyfields was quite a narrow street, running from Poplar High Street in the east, to West India Dock Rd in the west. It was at this end that the Chinese, most probably seamen and their families from the neighbouring docks, settled in the mid to late 1800's and opened their restaurants. The unique smells of their foods cooking carried in the air for quite a distance and it drew us kids toward it, like flies to honey.

The aromas of Cantonese dim-sum, Shanghai noodles, Sichuan chillies etc, wafted down through Pennyfields and although we were unaware of their origins, we knew, despite the fear that was instilled in us, we just had to go explore.

One warm summer evening in late August, possible 1953, temptation got the better of us, so throwing caution to the wind we set off for Chinatown. Little did we know what was instore for us.

It was one of those long, drawn-out summer nights with the twilight hanging in the air, for what felt like forever. As we moved towards Pennyfields the sun was a red glow in the west, leaving long shadows across Upper North Street. Looking west as we crossed East India Dock Rd the sun slipped below the horizon. This was the perfect night for our adventure, or so we thought! Passing Alfie Grove's newsstand on the corner of Saltwell St, then turning right opposite The White Horse Pub, Pennyfields beckoned us.

When you are aged 9 or 10, and you are with your two best mates, a good Cockney boy has no fear! Fear is not an option, however despite this I was personally scared half to death. Some of the stories I had heard were now looming large in my head, not to mention that I would not get home before dark, (which was almost upon us at the time), thereby guaranteeing , "a clip under the ear," from the old man. Despite this, we moved west down Pennyfields, hiding in the shadows close to the wall, as the distinctive smells of the Chinese food filled our nostrils.

The old buildings in the narrow street were in fact old terraced houses, most likely built in Victoria's reign, blackened by soot from years of exposure to coal fires, and "propped up," as a result of the bombing, they posed an ominous sight in the eerie half-light.

By now, panic was starting to overtake me, so I looked at my two fellow adventurers for a sign that we would abandon this stupidity and run for home as fast as we could. I have no doubt they were as frightened of what Chinatown might have in store for us, but none of us was going to show it, so we continued on. Each house, now used as a restaurant, had a basement below it and each basement had a very small widow, no more than a metre wide and 30 centimetre's in height. Now on our hands and knees, watching the front door for fear of a Chinese cook appearing, cleaver in hand, we made our way to the window, lay as flat to the ground as possible and waited in silence.

Try as we may, it was impossible to see anything through the windows. Most of the glass had been replaced with metal grills, and the remainder were painted on the inside. These Chinese did not want anyone to see what they were up to down there. Listening as hard as possible we could hear the sounds of men, loud men speaking, occasionally yelling and arguing in a strange language, none of which we could understand. Mixed in with all of this, we could clearly hear loud slapping sounds. Were they fighting? Why were they arguing and yelling? It was all a mystery to us kids, but fascination and fear kept us there, or was it something else?

As well as our hearing, another of our senses was working for us, and the sweet aroma coming through the metal grills was filling our lungs. I remember lying there, listening to those voices, the slapping sounds ringing in my ears, the odours of the Orient wafting around me and feeling like I was in some magical place, miles away from London's Eastend.

Without warning, a loud screeching sound came from the doorway. Standing there was a Chinese cook, complete with white apron, little white hat, white wellie boots, and I swear to this day, a very large cleaver in his hand.

Quickly shaking off the euphoria of the basement, we were on our feet in a split second, fear being the greatest motivator known to man, and we were off down Pennyfields, running as though our lives depended upon it, (perhaps they did!), with the rubber booted Chinaman in pursuit.

Now the good news is, a 9 year old Cockney boy can run much faster than a middle-aged Chinese cook in wellie boots, so as we approached the White Horse Pub, his screaming was growing less and less, but this did not stop the escape, or even slow it down. We ran across East India Dock Rd, dodging traffic and never dropped the pace until we were past the Sussex Arms, on the corner of Sussex and Upper North Street.

We split up at Ellesmere Street and despite struggling to breathe, I ran all the way home, the adventure behind me, and the old man waiting to give me that, "clip under the ear," that I knew I would get, (and did!).

It was years later that I finally discovered what it was that we had witnessed on that August night. The voices were not arguing or fighting, rather they were gambling. The "Slapping sounds," we heard so clearly were the sounds of the Mah-jong Tiles hitting the table, and of course that sweet, smoky exotic aroma we had enjoyed so much, was nothing less than Opium, brought in by the Chinese Sailors, and smoked in the now infamous, "Chinese Opium Dens."

With still 5 or so more years to wait until puberty, and without being aware of it at the time, I had experienced "getting high," from illegal drugs

Chapter 7.

A very smoky Christmas!

Adventures, like the one into Pennyfields, were many in the long days of summer. The school holidays started soon after the famous Wimbledon Tennis Tournament, and continued for six to eight weeks, depending on which school you attended.

As us kids grew older, the adventures became even more daring and often, although we did not realise it at the time, they became downright dangerous.

One bright summer evening, possibly around 9 pm, I was home, sitting in our little living room, with all the windows open in an attempt to keep the house cool, when there was a very loud knock on the front door. This was most unusual, because in those days we never locked our door, and it was usual for visitors to simply open the door, yell out their name, and walk straight in.

I rushed to the door, beating Mum by a whisker and opened it, only to find two of my best mates, standing there looking very frightened. As Mum approached, one of them yelled as loud as he could, "Mrs Smith, your Bobby is on top of the Church!"

Pushing straight past me, Mum ran out into the street, looked to her right, and what she saw froze her to the spot. My brother, Bob had climbed from the ground, up the side of the nearest of the two brick walls. He had managed to climb up what was originally the front of St Gabriel's, but had then moved onto the large heavy timber, that had once been the main support for the roof apex. He had straddled this timber, and in a series of moves, made his way out, until he was sitting halfway between the front and back walls of the bombed ruin, his legs dangling, one each side of the highest point left standing, more than 30 metres above the old church floor.

I have no idea what was going on inside my poor Mother's head, but to see her eldest son in that precarious position must have taken at least 10 years off of her life. By this time, Bob was waving down at her, obviously very proud of his achievement.

Mum walked, (yes walked not run), across Chrisp St, and up what was left of the old church steps. She walked through the old doorway, looked up, and said, quite simply and in a normal tone of voice, "come down from there, and be careful!" To her absolute horror, Bob pushed himself up and in one movement, stood up and turned to face the direction from which he had come.

Too scared to say anything it case it might scare him, Mum could just watch, and I suspect pray that he would not fall. He balanced himself, and just as if he were some kind of high wire act from a visiting Circus, he walked all the way to the front wall, dropped down onto it, and successfully climbed back down to the ground, much to the great relief of poor old Mum. When your neighbourhood is derelict houses, bombed factories and churches, this is where you played. Bob could see no harm or danger, and was very surprised when the old man punished him!

Another great adventure included the old ammo dump, plus the Poplar to Stratford railway line.

In Chrisp St, opposite Godalming Rd and next to Flays shop, surrounded by a high chain net fence with barbed wire on the top was the old ammo dump. All the kids knew it was there, but we were never sure what was stored under the Army green tarpaulin sheets, sitting there in full view. The gate leading into this mysterious plot of land, was fastened shut by a huge padlock, that bore the letters, W.D.

with and arrow facing upwards, separating these two letters.

It seems that towards the middle of the war, the government were concerned what might happen, should the Nazi's cross the English Channel and mount an attack. In preparation for such an event, various forms of ammunition were scattered all over the south of England. Our little, "ammo dump," in Chrisp Street was one of those, and it contained all sorts of, "goodies," as us kids referred to the wooden boxes, hidden under the covers.

Now to any kid who lived in the east end at that time, fences were viewed as a deterrent to enter, rather they were seen as a challenge to be attacked and conquered, so it was no surprise that the perimeter was breached and various dangerous articles were in the possession of 8 & 9 year old boys!

One such possession was a small round metal object, about the size of a large men's wristwatch, with a piece of strap iron protruding from each side. These were in fact detonator's, small explosive devices, that made a very loud bang, if crushed.

To this day I have no idea as what these wonderful, dangerous things were used for, by their owners, I.E. the Military, but us kids did know what we would use them for. Running off of Chrisp Street was a cul-de-sac, Cording Street, which had a very high wall at the end, behind which was the old Poplar to Stratford railway line. Today it is part of the DLR, or Docklands Light Rail, however in the early fifties it was used purely for goods trains, steam powered locomotives, with an engine driver and fireman on board. The rails were still in disrepair as a result of the bombing, so the trains would travel slowly past the big wall, and it was there we would have our fun!

One of us, (usually the tallest), would be helped up onto the top of the wall. He would then lean down and help a second up onto the top. In a reverse of this move, one boy would be lowered down the other side and onto the small embankment on the side of the railway. Taking care that a train was not coming down the line, and receiving the all-clear from the lookout on top of the wall, one of the detonators would be placed upon the railway line, with the two metal straps bent to hold it in place, before a hasty retreat was made, a return to the wall and a hoist up, ready for the fun to begin. All that was needed was the next train. Lying flat on top of the wall, hoping we would not be seen, it was usually a short wait. The train duly arrived, with the driver hanging out of the side window to see ahead. Watching from our advantage point, we would see the heavy iron wheel of the engine, approach and then crush the detonator. The subsequent explosion was, to put it mildly, very loud, and was in very close proximity our unsuspecting engine driver, scaring the daylights out of the poor man. We kids dropped back down off of the wall, and very quickly took-off for home, delighted with ourselves! Another enjoyable sunny summers day in post-war Poplar. Soon after the school holidays finished and the clocks moved back, denoting English summertime was over, the days drew shorter and the weather quickly changed. The old North Wind blew into East London, bringing with it the cold and damp days that typified a desolate winter. Even with all of this happening around us, we kids did not give a brass razoo for any of it. Winter among the bombed ruins and cleared bombed properties was just as much fun! Sometime around the middle of October, the scavenging for firewood began. On the corner of Ellesmere Street and Godalming Road, the temporary bomb shelter from 1941 had been removed, leaving the perfect place for our bonfire. At the same time, an old pram was found, in preparation for the old sack of rags, mask and hat, aptly became our version of Guy Fawkes.

"Remember, remember the fifth of November!" Guy Fawkes night, held in remembrance of the failed Gunpowder Plot of 1605, against the British Government was fast approaching, so it was time to take our Guy Fawkes out, and respectfully request money from the public. "Penny for the Guy mister?" was the catch cry and all monies raised would be spent on Fireworks, purchased by an adult in the Toy Bazaar, Loaders or Chriton's, depending on who had the lowest prices.

Poplar had more than its share of wood laying around the place, courtesy of Adolf Hitler and his Luftwaffe. The timbers that were retrieved from the destroyed houses, factories, churches etc. were old, dry and burnt beautifully. The challenge was to see who could build the biggest fire or, "Bonnie," as we called them. Old wooden doors, floorboards, you name it, they were all piled up, waiting for the big night. Despite having houses on all three sides of the debris, the fire was lit around 4.30pm and the fireworks, including rockets that zoomed into the sky, roman candles that us kids would hold as they fizzed & popped their sparkles, Catharine wheels that were nailed to a nearby fence, and once lit, spun around showering flame and colour everywhere, but everyone's favourite, (well, mine at least), was, "The Penny Banger." No fancy colours, no flight, no spinning, just a very loud, "Bang!" The instructions on this firework were simple and clear: "light blue touch paper and retire." Now where was the fun in that? We did it Cockney style.

Light blue touch paper, wait for it to start fizzing, then throw it at the feet of one of the girls!!!!!!!!!!!!!! Wait for the explosion, watch the girls run and scream, and laugh our heads off, until someone threw one behind us, and then it was our turn to panic!! Poplar Hospital was always very busy on November 5th! The fire was so big, it would still be glowing red hot, the next morning. How we never burnt down the entire neighbourhood is still a mystery to me. Despite the noise, the danger and the pollution etc. it is sad that this great tradition is gone.

Once bonfire night was behind us, and the weather grew increasing more unfriendly, we focussed on the next big thing………. Christmas!

As a resident of Australia for more than 50 years, I have gotten used to Christmas being celebrated on hot weather, with cold seafood, and even colder beer! Not so in London. Christmas time was always accompanied by cold & damp weather. Fog would often greet us as we woke on

Christmas morning. It was a far different affair than Christmas today.

Our little living room in number 46, was very small indeed. Small table, up against the wall, with newspaper for a tablecloth. Two small wooden armed chairs, one each side of the fireplace, candlesticks on the mantlepiece, with the clock my Father had built from parts he purchased at Hodges Watch & Clock shop, completed the room.

In winter, the most important, (and best as far as I was concerned), was the coal fire. It was warm & magical, and sitting beside it on a cold winters night, listening to, The Archers," & "Lost in Space," on the radio was everything a boy could want.

The fireplace was cleaned every day, the ashes removed, hearth swept, before yesterday's newspaper was scrunched up into tight balls, placed onto the fire grill, ready for the next cold London night. On top of the paper was placed kindling, or "sticks," as we called them, "chopped up," from wood from the surrounding debris, in the backyard every Sunday morning, and kept dry in the Scullery, ready for use when required.

Coming down the stairs in the winter mornings was a very cold affair. Leaving behind the warm bed and entering the fireless living room was no fun, but it was all we knew. On Christmas Day, 1948 the weather was at its worst. Heavy mist, accompanied by freezing fog covered England and when my brother woke me, slightly before 5.00am, on that cold Christmas morning, it was 5 degrees below freezing outside, however the excitement of what was waiting in the living room downstairs, overruled the temptation to stay in the warm bed. As silently as possible, and avoiding the stairs that, from experience we knew would creak if we stepped upon them, we crept down the stairs, into the living room and closed the door behind us.

Our living room was decorated for Christmas, not with sparkling lights, nor with a well-lit Christmas tree. No holly or mistletoe. If such things existed in 1948, the Smiths could not afford them. Instead we made, "Paper Chains,". These were all made by us in the lead-up to the holiday, using strips of coloured paper, made into a loop, and glued from the glue pot sitting on the side of the fire to melt . Each strip was carefully glued, and looped together. Four chains were made, and then suspended from the centre of the room to each corner.

As we sat underneath these, we started to open our presents. It was only 18months after "Rationing," finished in the UK and many items were still hard to get. Our Christmas that year consisted of one present each, usually a toy that our Father had made and kept hidden from us. In addition we always got one apple & one orange each, plus a boiled sweet & a toffee.

Looking back now, it would be easy to believe that we were disappointed, or upset by these presents, but that would be far from true. We loved Christmas, and everything it brought with it. We knew that Dad had purchased a, "Capon Chicken," in Chrisp Street market on Christmas Eve. We would enjoy a Christmas Dinner that day, with our little family. Dad had told us that on one of his trips into the

West India Dock, he had bought, "Blancmange," and although we had no idea as to what that was, it sounded great. We had never had custard at that time, so Blancmange sounded very posh, and that was special indeed.

Sitting on the floor with our presents, the clock approaching 5.30 am, my brother came up with a plan to make Mum & Dad happy at Christmas.

"Let's light the fire for them!"

I agreed with this, as it would save poor old Dad from having to do it when he came down, plus it would warm the room, which at that time of the morning was freezing.

We quickly scrunched up the newspaper, laid it in the hearth and put a shovel of coal on top. Using a match from the Bryant & Mays matchbox, the paper was ignited, and we sat back and waited for the fire to grow and send out that lovely warm glow. Sadly this did not happen!

The paper burned well, and some of the sticks began to show small flames, however, us kids were completely unaware of the fact that fire needs oxygen. The coal we had included was premature, and the "fire," was dying in front of our eyes.

Now two Cockney boys don't give up that easy. This fire could be saved, but how? My brother knew exactly what to do. "I've seen Dad do this," he said and with that he opened a full page of the old newspaper, and like putting a curtain in front of a window, he placed the newspaper across the entire fireplace. Within seconds, the fire began to burn. As the draft went under the bottom of the newspaper and fed the flames, a roaring sound could be heard, and the light coming from behind the newspaper grew brighter & brighter.

"I told you this would work," said Bob, very pleased with himself. Dad was going to be very happy with his two sons. Suddenly, without warning, the newspaper began to burn. In less than a second it was blazing, and still being held by Bob. "Shit," he said, and without any hesitation, pushed the flaming paper into the fire, and up, into the chimney.

Now all was well at this point, The fire was burning well. The heat was starting to fill the room and we were very happy with ourselves, but unfortunately this state of euphoria was short lived. Within a couple of minutes of the newspaper disappearing into the chimney, very large pieces of red hot burning soot began to fall into the fire, many of them rolling out into the hearth, very close to us. Bob grabbed the coal shovel and began to shovel up pieces of the smoking hot soot, and return them to the fire, however as quick as he did so, more, even bigger, hotter and smokier soot arrived like missiles into our living room. Mum & dad were oblivious to all of this, still sound asleep upstairs, until a very loud noise from the front door woke them. Who knocks on someone's door at 5.30 am on Christmas morning?

As fate would have it, our neighbour, Mr Freeman was a bus driver, and he was on his way to work, but as he slowly navigated his way through the fog, he was surprised to find very large, red hot glowing soot bombs falling all around him. Peering up through the fog, he saw the chimney, now with flames coming out of the top.

When we opened our front door, to determine who was knocking at this un-godly hour, a very nervous Mr Freeman explained that our chimney was on fire, and should he get the fire brigade? Bob was very quick with his reply, "it's not our chimney Mr Freeman. It must be next door's!"

A well placed, bare-faced lie might well have worked, but not this time. The ruckus had woken Dad, and arriving into the living room, still in his vest and long-johns, he was greeted by the mayhem that we had caused.

Dad had been a volunteer fireman in London during the war, so putting out fires was not new to him. He filled two saucepans with water, and on his hands & knees in front to the hearth, he used an old tin mug to throw this water up, into the chimney, in the hope of extinguishing the flames. The soot continued to fall, but it was now black, not red, and was cooler. The fire was under control, but our living room was getting blacker and smokier by the minute. Eventually the fire was out. Dad had opened the window to let the smoke out, (and the cold air in!), and Bob & I had made ourselves a large piece of toast each, both of which were covered in strawberry jam. As we sat on one of the armchairs, looking down at Dad, trying to clean up the black filthy mess we had made, he suddenly turned around to look at both of us. His face was completely black from the soot, as was his white vest. I was petrified. After all, we had caused all of this, and retribution was sure to come, but hopefully not today, Christmas Day? Bob however saw the

funny side of it. Just prior to taking a huge bite from is slice of toast, he made a remark to Dad, suggesting Dad looked like a, "Sooty Santa Claus." Clearly not appreciating the humour of the situation, Dad swung a quick and well-aimed back hander at Bob, catching him just as the toast was going into his mouth. The strawberry jam laden slice flew out of Bob's hand, and hit the wall behind, but before doing so, it spread a layer of butter & jam across Bob's face.
It was at this time Mum came downstairs. Our intention had been for her and Dad to find a warm & welcoming Christmas morning. What she found was arguably the furthest thing from it. It was not the best start to the day; however, it was Christmas. The mess was cleaned up. Bob had received his retribution, (I had escaped mine), the dinner was cooked, and we even had that Blancmange with Christmas Pudding for, "afters," (dessert to you posh people). Christmas 1948…. One to remember!

Chapter 8.

Banana's, Bedbugs & the Big Noise!

As kids in Poplar, we neither understood, nor cared as to how things were done by our, "Oldie's." We knew they did not have a lot of money, and they worked hard, but that was the full extent of our understanding.
My Dad used to drive a lorry for a living. On the front of his, "Scammell Lorry," clearly printed were the words, "Chas. Poulter Transport, The Highway, Limehouse E14."

Having left Thomas Street School, at the age of 14, he found himself in a world badly affected by the great depression. Work was very scarce, especially for a boy with minimal education.

He started his first job as a delivery boy for Copping's Smallgoods in Chrisp Street. Riding the exact same model of bicycle, made famous by David Jason, or "Granville," as Ronnie Barker referred to him, in the TV show, "Open all Hours," Dad would deliver hams, cheese etc to all parts East London.

At the age of 16, he became a lorry driver, but things were a lot different in the transport industry then, compared to today. In the very cold winters of the mid -twenties, just getting the lorries moving was a feat in itself. Electric starter motors were unheard of at that time. Instead, the cold stiff diesel engine had to be started by hand. To achieve this, the following process was followed, every morning.

At 4.00am, Dad would arrive at the yard, and find the one lorry that had been left, fully loaded from the night before. This was the one he would have to get running first. The second step was to pour some diesel fuel over some paper and sticks, place this mixture under the engine of said lorry, and proceed to set it alight. Now this may sound like a strange & dangerous thing to do, and indeed it was not without danger, however the temperature of the oil in the sump of the diesel engine was approximately 32 degrees Fahrenheit, and at that temperature, it was so thick, that the starting handle to be used to start the engine, could not be rotated. The fire was simply to, "warm her up a bit," so the handle could be turned.

After sufficient time had passed, and the fire had done its job, it was time to begin. He would place the long, heavy starting handle, through the hole in the front bumper, then through the guide hole, so that the pins on the front of it, engaged into the sprocket on the engine. Even with the engine being nice & warm it still required a tremendous effort to turn the handle, and get the engine turning over. The four cylinder diesel engine was just too strong, due the very high compression, found in such a beast. In order to do this, each cylinder had a, "de-compression valve," located on the top. All four valves needed to be opened, in order for the driver, (my Dad in this case), to, "turn her over." At this point he would have been joined by another driver, and once Dad had the motor turning over, his mate would close one of the four valves. If all had gone to plan, the engine would begin to, "fire," on this one cylinder. Still turning the handle to keep up the momentum, and after a few seconds had passed, a second valve was closed, and hopefully the engine would continue to run, (albeit on two cylinders) until it was sufficiently warm enough to close the remaining two valves, after which, "Geronimo," one lorry engine running.

As soon as the engine was up to temperature, this fully-loaded-lorry would be used to "push start" all of the lorry's in the yard, in order to get them ready for the drivers to leave the yard by the 8.0 o'clock start time.

Dad worked a 12 hour day, finishing at 4.0 pm, 6 days a week. He was a lorry driver until 1952, when he left to work in the Docks.

Canary Wharf as we know it today, is a testament to foresight & ingenuity of modern man. I can assure you it is a far cry from the Canary Wharf of 1952, when my father worked there as a, "Casual Tally Clerk,"

In those days, Canary Wharf was a part of the Port of London Authority owned, West India Docks.

Together with the Millwall Dock, it was one of the busiest docks in the world, giving employment to thousands of East-Enders. For close to 180 years, this area was filled with the hustle & bustle of ships being loaded & unloaded, bringing cargoes from all over the world, to post-war-Britain. Canary Wharf was in fact, "Number 32 berth of the West Wood Quay," situated in the Import Dock. Built in 1936 for, "Fruit Lines," a subsidiary of Fred Olsen Shipping. The Canary Islands, situated of the coast of north-western Africa, was an easy sea journey for the Olsen Line ships, and the fruit to be found there was ideal for the tables of Britain.

Fully loaded with banana's they would head north following the coastlines of Portugal & Spain, crossing the infamous Bay of Biscay, into the English Channel, and dock at Canary Wharf.

Each morning, Dad would leave home on his old black pushbike, and by 7.00am, he would be at the gates on the West India Docks, standing with all the other casual workmen, hoping to get, "picked-up," for a day's work. This practice took place every morning, six days per week, and was referred to by the locals as, "Standing on the Stones," due to the fact that the road outside of the two large dock gates was made of large granite stones, known as "Cobble stones." Built in the 1800's to withstand the iron rims of horse drawn carts and steel horseshoes of the mighty Clydesdale's pulling them.

Standing on the stones one cold dark morning, my father told me that a horse and cart passed through the gates, and there were sparks coming off of the horseshoes as they clipped against the granite.

At 7.00am, some Port of London men would arrive at the dock gates. Depending on how many ships had made it into the port, men would be chosen to pass through the gates, and earn a day's pay. Stevedores, lighterman, dockhands, and Tally Clerks were picked, and when the process was complete, those not chosen, returned home, no work that day!

Despite leaving school at such a young age, my father was naturally gifted with numbers. In the "pre-calculator-electronics age," everything was done with a clipboard & pencil. His great skill with numbers meant he was picked most days, and he spent many, many days, tallying the banana's as they were unloaded. He would arrive home at night, and the smell of those banana's would fill the house. I can honestly say that banana's and the Canary Wharf, put food on our table for many years.

Our little house in Ellesmere Street was a miracle in itself. Basically it was a dump, a clean, well-loved and well cared for, but none the less a dump. The rooms were really very small, the door on the cupboard under the stairs was always open, the simple reason being that it was twisted & distorted by the bombing, it was impossible to close. Despite all of this, Cockneys always had their pride! I can never remember my father leaving the house without his collar & tie. His shirt was old, as were all of his clothes, most likely purchased at Shkolnik's second-hand clothes shop, but pride meant always looking your best. Our house was always clean. Mum looked after the place like it was a palace, even though it was owned by others, and we paid rent. Our clothes were clean, our beds were clean, until that is.............Bedbugs!

The family next door, were also a family of four, with the eldest child being a girl. Their bedroom was next to ours, with just a dividing brick wall between us. One morning, it was summer and had been a very hot night, I woke up to go to school, as per usual. My brother's bed was only a few feet away from mine in our small back bedroom, and he looked at me with wide-eyed fear. I looked at myself to see what he was so concerned about, only to see thousands of red spots up both arms. Crying and very scared, I went downstairs to find Mum, who after removing all of my clothes found more red spots, everywhere, (and I MEAN everywhere).

Not knowing what the cause was, Mum kept me home from school, and at 9.00am, she did something that was rarely done in those days. She took me to the doctors.

Although the National Health Service began in 1948, payment to a doctor was still a reality, and not many people could afford it. As such we did not go very often, but on this occasion, there I was, standing in Doctor Lowe's Alton Street surgery, stark naked. After careful examination, the diagnosis was clear. Bedbug bites, from top to toe. Mum gave me a silver sixpence to give to the doctor, and in return we left with a very large, (well to me it was), bottle of Calamine Lotion. On return home, I was again stripped, and painted with the pink lotion, very embarrassing, but, however not as embarrassed as Mum. For her to have bedbugs in her house was something she could not accept, also if the neighbours found out, she would become the gossips target for weeks to come. How did we get bedbugs in the house? This was both unacceptable & unbelievable. "Your father will get to the bottom of this, when he gets home from work," she told me and although I had not done anything wrong, (in fact I was the victim), I was still a bit scared of what might happen.

Later in the day, my bed was stripped of its bedclothes, and the mattress was covered in small brown-coloured bugs. She was completely correct when she said Dad would know what to do. Without hesitation, he mixed up a bucket of water, with a small amount of copper sulphate, purchased from Boots the chemist in Chrisp Street. He poured this on the floor under and around my bed, and "splashed," the remainder on the mattress. He told my brother & I that this would kill all of the bugs, and the blue colour would gradually fade from the mattress. "This boys, is where the expression, Blue Murder came from!" To this day I have no idea if he was correct, but he was right about it killing the bugs.

The next step was to, "track down the cause," It was very obvious the bugs had somehow made their way through or over the adjoining wall from number 48, next door.

Dad knocked on their door, and when the lady of the house appeared, he told her what had happened. She denied that it could be from their house, but when the man of the house appeared and agreed with her, the old man did what any good cockney would do. He entered the small passageway, and when the man attempted to stop him, he quickly & firmly shoved him out of the way, and went up the stairs, into the back bedroom.

It seems that the girl, whose bed was against the adjoining wall, was, in fact a bed wetter The room smelt badly of urine plus the bed was both wet and dirty. It seems the girl had a problem, over which she had little or no control. Her mother, however, was too lazy to clean, simply pulling the bedsheets back, and putting the child into the same bed each night.

Another lady & neighbour who lived across the road from us, was related to the girl's mother, and when she heard about the situation, she and a friend, went in and cleaned the whole house, after which she apologised to Mum, Dad & I. They kept a vigilant eye on number 48 after that and we never had bedbugs in the house again.

Copper Sulphate, Calamine lotion plus a good hard shove from Dad fixed the problem.......permanently.

Following this little episode, Dad decided that I should get some sort of recognition, for being so brave and, as he put it, "not winging & whining about it!"

My treat was to be a trip with Dad, into the West India Docks, where I would see all the big ships up close, meet all of his mates, and maybe go the, "Caff," (Café), for tea & toast. On the day chosen I was so excited to be going on such an adventure. To me this was heaven. Nothing I could ever imagine would be its equal.

Dad wheeled his big black bike backwards, out through the front door, then putting his bicycle clips on the bottom of his trousers, he sat on. My place was on the crossbar, so up I went, and we set off. Riding down Upper North Street, then Pennyfields, (not scared of the Chinese cooks this time), into West India Dock Road, and straight through the dock gates, giving the policeman on duty there, a big wave as we went through. Riding on a steel crossbar, on cobbled streets, crossing railway tracks was a very bumpy affair, but I did not care in the least. I was amazed at the size of the big cargo ships, with their multi-coloured funnels, with stars on some, palm trees on others. It was amazing. But there was still more to come.

As came down towards the quayside, we stopped to talk to a man that Dad knew. When I looked at him, his face seemed familiar to me. He said hello and gave me a penny, to spend later. His name was Bygraves and he was in fact the performer, Max Bygrave's brother. I remember him telling me he could sing better than his brother Max. Not sure if that was correct, but I was very happy to spend the penny he gave me, on a penny ice lolly in Crosses shop, when I returned to Ellesmere street, later that day.

The hustle & bustle of the Docks was unbelievable. The cranes were like giraffe's, with their long jibs going up into the sky and the shorter part on the top, bobbing up & down. They would drop their hooks down into the bowels of the ships, and as I stood and watched, enthralled by this organised mayhem, the hook would appear, carrying all sorts of goods, from wherever the ship had been. Frozen lambs covered in white cloth, with, "Canterbury Lamb, NZ,' stamped on the side. Wooden barrels, often six or more at a time might appear, with perhaps, rum from the West Indies or Port from Portugal. A wooden raft, connected from each corner to the hook, with wooden crates, all stacked neatly and evenly with the words, "Carlsberg Pilsner, Copenhagen Denmark."

I saw these wooden rafts dropped by the cranes onto funny looking little trolleys. They were flat at the back, with the word, "Lister," on the side. The driver stood at the front, and as soon as his load was onboard, he would operate the handles behind his back, and off he would go, no sooner moving away before he was replaced by another funny looking trolley. It was like it was all driven by clockwork. I stood there, absolutely dumbstruck. It was the highlight of my life until that point, and more than sixty years later, I still enjoy the memories.

As we stood looking at all of this amazing stuff, I heard a familiar sound from behind. My Dad's two brothers, both of whom were Tally Clerks for the Port of London Authority, had arrived. Uncle John, dad's youngest brother was a survivor of the British exodus from Dunkirk, on the French Coast. One of the 338,000 Servicemen to be evacuated from the harbour and beaches and return home safely, only to be sent back to fight for his country, until he was, "demobbed from the Services," in 1945.

The other brother was the eldest, Uncle Will, or as he was more generally known throughout the Eastend, "The Big Noise." He was in fact, a very big man, not so tall, but big & solidly built. He was a chronic asthmatic, so much so that he failed the medical for the Army, and was assigned the role of, "Essential War Worker." It was this role that saw him driving a London Transport Bus, for the major part of the war. He was also a volunteer fire fighter, spending many hours and days, putting out fires caused by the bombing, all over greater London.

One day, when I was around eighteen years old, I asked my father, "why was Uncle Will called the big noise?" As a part of my growing up in the Eastend, and as a tribute of respect to the thousands of characters that have come from there, here is the story of the big noise, as told to me on that day.

Essential war work was considered to be any job that kept the UK functioning during those dark times. In uncle Will's case, it was driving a bus through the streets of London, helping people to travel for essential reasons, such as getting to & from their place of work.

One day in the summer of 1943, an altercation began on the footpath, just outside of Selfridges Department Store. It seems that three young men had attempted to steal from the store, and upon being discovered, ran out of the store, and unfortunately for them, straight into the arms of a policeman.

At the same time as this was occurring, Uncle Will was at the wheel of his bus, heading west. Coming across this scene, he saw that the policeman was putting up a gallant battle with the three men, however he was struggling, and was in danger of being hurt and therefore failing to apprehend the would-be thieves.

Will immediately stopped his bus, and as he jumped from the cabin, he took the large steel starting handle from behind the seat, and crossed Oxford street. Still with the benefit of surprise on his side, he swung this, "make-shift-weapon," at the leg of one of the perpetrators, causing him to fall to the ground. The other two were by now, getting the advantage of the policeman, however, before they realised that help had arrived, Will swung again, this time landing his trusty starting handle on the shinbone of the alleged thief. Writhing in pain, he too fell to the ground, leaving Will to assist the lone policeman to arrest the third. It was all over in a matter of seconds; however Will was very much the hero of the day. A police sergeant, who arrived after the melee was over, thanked Will and took his bus drivers number, plus his name & address.

Will then left the scene, and as only a cheeky cockney can, he took a bow to the standing ovation he received from the passengers on his bus.

Some months later, Will was invited to attend a ceremony at Mansion House, where he was duly presented with a Certificate of Valour, and a letter from the Lord Mayor of London, thanking him for his meritorious bravery.

After the war ended and London began to rebuild, Uncle Will changed from driving a bus, to driving an articulated lorry, for British Road Services, (BRS). Experienced drivers were at a premium, as a result of the war, and driving such a vehicle around the streets of London, was an art in itself. One which Will knew well, but sometimes did not adhere to: Sometime in the late 1940's, (I think 1947), Will was assigned a job that required all of his skills and experience. He was to go to an address, in North London, (somewhere near Southgate I believe). The story, as relayed to me was that the owner of the house where Will was sent, was moving to Australia. Most of his furniture & possessions were already packed and in transit, however, he was also taking his prized possession, that being a full-size-grand-piano. Uncle Will's job, was to load this onto the flat trailer of his lorry, and take it to the Royal Docks at Silvertown, (the very docks that he would become a Tally Clerk later in his life).

I have no knowledge as to how this expensive and delicate musical instrument was loaded onto the lorry, but according to the story I was told, (and as was usual for that era), it was Will's responsibility to secure his load, before starting his journey south. Locking the wheels that supported the weight of the piano, was first, followed by a series of ropes, and blankets, to hold & protect fine finish on the piano legs.

Will took his time and checked every rope carefully, and when satisfied that the piano was firmly attached to his lorry, he headed for the A10, the main road back to London. With plenty of time, (or so he believed), Will followed the road signs, and driving with caution, made his way through Tottenham, crossing the famous, "White Hart Lane," home ground of Tottenham Hotspurs Football Club, then passing Bruce Castle, with its magnificent blue clock face, situated in Tottenham's oldest public park. He knew all of these roads well, having driven on the many times in the past, so he was very comfortable, enjoying his driving experience. The traffic was heavy, but was moving steadily, as Will passed the magnificent St Ignatius Catholic Church on his right hand side. It was at this point that things started to go wrong. The traffic slowed dramatically, and Will found himself behind a long line of vehicles, now moving at a walking pace. It took him a few minutes to realise that he come up behind a Funeral Procession. A long & very slow Funeral Procession.

Taking all of this into consideration, knowing the roads ahead of him and being aware of the time, Will made a decision. He knew he was about to go up the incline known as Stamford Hill, not a huge incline, but steep & long enough to slow his piano-laden truck down. Even so, he could definitely go faster than this snail's pace he found himself in, so he made his move.

Changing down to the lowest gear in his lorry, Will put his right hand out of the window, pulled down on the steering wheel, and began his ascent of Stamford Hill, in the right-hand-lane. Slowly but steadily accelerating onto the beginning of the hill, Will wanted to get as much speed as possible, so he would not slow down those following him. By the time he reached the start of the hill, his speedometer was registering just over 20 miles-per-hour, a very good speed for any lorry in 1947. The vehicles dawdling along on his left changed from a random mix, to shiny black funeral cars, with attendee's in the back, and a chauffeur in the front, all dressed in black, and all looking very sombre. Will expected to pass about 6 or 7 of these cars, then pass the hearse itself, after which he could return to the safety of the left lane, however, circumstances that day were far from the expectations of my dear uncle.

The Funeral Procession that he had chosen to, "speed past," was no ordinary one. It was in fact the funeral of a long & well respected local Costermonger, who had begun his career selling fruit & vegetables from a handcart, and grew this humble beginning into a highly successful chain of shops that crossed England from north to south. He left this earth a very rich man, and his funeral was a special occasion. There was 25-plus cars for mourners, 6 more for family, 2 more for immediate family. In front of all of these was the hearse itself. A hearse befitting a famous and well-loved Costermonger.

A large carriage with highly polished spoke wheels, carried the gold embossed coffin, which was clearly visible through the engraved glass sides. Flowers were present on all four sides of the casket, with more covering the entire top. Sitting immediately in front of this were the two coachmen, dressed appropriately in black ties, black silk high hats, reins held firmly in the driver's hands, they made an awesome sight as they passed the bystanders on Stamford Hill, who in turn, stopped and stood in silence, hats removed and hands on hearts. The six black horses pulling the hearse were decked out to perfection, their coats groomed to a fine shine, leather & brass polished on their harness. On top of each of their heads was a large plume of black feathers.

Walking slowly, just a yard or two ahead was the Funeral Director himself, also in black from top to toe, he wore a black silk scarf, which flowed back from his neck & hat. The final adornment was the black silk sash, worn around his waist as an accreditation to his rank & importance. Apart from the low purring of the funeral cars, Stamford Hill was as silent as it could ever be. This magnificent site, reminiscent of the days of Victoria & Albert was a sight to behold!

Uncle Will, in his BRS lorry, now travelling at close to 25 miles per hour, had not foreseen such a long procession. He certainly had not considered it, but he was travelling very well, he would eventually pass, then he could continue on, the Royal Dock Gates open, ready to receive his load. He continued up the hill, but he was yet to see the hearse, and his opportunity to change lanes & slow down.

Will knew that he had a number of different routes he could follow, any of which would get him to his destination, however, this delay was causing a time pressure. He had to follow the quickest route, and this meant moving into the left lane as soon as possible.

After what seemed an eternity, the hearse, with its six black horses came into view. Not wishing to miss his turn, Will kept pressure on the accelerator of his lorry, and eventually passed the hearse, passed the director, then, took the opportunity to re-join the left lane. Will pulled the wheel to the left, only to realise that he was already level with Clapton Common, the road he needed to be on if he was to make his timetable. He pulled even harder on the wheel, the lorry now broadside to the hearse, and believing he had made it, Will pressed down, yet again on the accelerator, feeling very pleased with himself.

Now comes the reason uncle Will became, "The Big Noise." The ropes he had used to secure the piano were solidly and safely tied to the legs and they did their job. As the forces of kinetic energy hit the piano, it did not want to go around the corner into Clapton Common, rather it tried its very best to continue up Stamford Hill, and that is exactly what it did.

The lorry with all three of the piano's legs, still firmly attached went left. The piano, minus its legs, went straight on, until another force, that of gravity took over, and the piano crashed down on the road.

Some days later, passers-by who had been standing, head bowed watching this solemn and silent funeral pass, stated that the noise made by the piano drop as, "what I imagine the noise would be, standing in the belfry when Big Ben struck," It must have been something like this, because the horses pulling the hearse reared up, and clearly spooked, set off into a gallop, the coachmen on the top desperately trying to control their charges and the Funeral Director diving into the gutter in an attempt to avoid being trampled and killed.

A Newspaper, published later that week reported that the hearse, (yes……and the Costermonger) bolted at full speed, and reached Balls Pond Road in Dalston before being brought under control.

Uncle Will was arrested!

When the time came for Will to appear in court, the newspapers had lost interest, the Costermonger had been buried, (eventually) and BRS had fired him. He was well aware that he could face time in Gaol, or a very big fine, and/or a loss of his driving licence. His fears were very real as he stood in the dock, and awaited his fate!

As expected, the judge was not at all sympathetic, and once all the charges were read, he looked sternly at Will, then asked him the question, "do you have anything to say in your defence." What could he possibly say that might save him? Was there anything at all?

Will stood in the dock. He began by apologising to the Costermongers family and all other attendees in the procession. He apologised to the police and the council workers who cleaned up the remains of the grand piano. He finally apologised to the court, then he took a package from his pocket. Slowly opening the envelope inside, he took out the Certificate of Valour he had received years earlier for his part in the robbery at Selfridges and placed it on the rail in front of him.

He then read the letter from the Lord Mayor of London out loud and when he had finished, he appealed to the judge to take these actions into account.

The judge asked to see both documents and after taking the time to read them, passed sentence. Will was found guilty on all charges, but was dismissed without penalty due to his previous public service. He left court, a free man, no fines, and no Certificate of Valour.

The Eastend produced many such characters back in the day, my Uncle Wiil being one of them.

"The Big Noise," was a true Cockney Character indeed.

Chapter 9.

Elsie Daisy Smith.

Elsie Daisy Smith, (Nee Hayes), was born in January, 1910, the first of eight children. She was not born a Cockney, in fact she was a "Kentish Lass," from the south side of the River Thames, Gravesend. Gravesend got its name from the time of the "Great Plague," that spread through London in 1665, killing an estimated 100,000 people, approximately one quarter of the population of Londoners at that time. The Plague raged for almost 18 months, and "Body Carriers," with horse and carts travelled the streets with the now infamous call of, "bring out your dead!"

Bodies were buried everywhere in London, usually in mass graves, but many were taken down river on the outgoing tides and buried along the banks. Gravesend was as far as the graves spread.

At age 9, her father died in a work accident, whereby he fell into the hold of a ship, while working as a Stevedore. As a result, together with her mother, and two younger siblings, she moved to the southeast London suburb of Lewisham. With no male to earn, money was scarce, and they struggled, just to eat and survive. The consequence of this caused my grandmother to make a decision. Elsie would be, "put into service," so in 1920, just after the end of World War 1, she moved into a grand house on Shooters Hill, living at the back of the house and filling the position of, "Scullery Maid." She was later promoted to, "Upstairs Maid," and looked after the Captain's children, then in 1922 he was transferred to India. He requested Elsie go with him and his family, however, grandmother refused, and Elsie returned to Coldbath Street in Lewisham.

Of course she needed to earn money, (she now had three stepsister's and a stepbrother all of whom needed to be fed), so she became a, "Fruit-Peeler," preparing the oranges & lemons for jams & marmalades at the Robertson's factory in nearby Catford.

I do not know how my parents met, but in 1938 they married and moved into 46 Ellesmere St, Poplar, two doors from where Dad was born and raised.

Like it or not, Mum was living in the Eastend, and had no choice other than to become a Cockney? She never did!

Despite spending 27 years there, Mum remained a, "Kentish Lass," until she passed away in Sydney Australia in 1990.

In 1946, after the war ended and East London, like the rest of the UK was trying to rebuild and get back to normal, Elsie, my Mum became pregnant with her third child, and in the last few hours of that year, she gave birth to a baby girl, Margaret Patricia Smith.

She returned to Ellesmere Street with Margaret. Dad was delighted with his two sons and brand new daughter. He immediately began to make toys for all three of us, and his choice for Margaret was a dolls pram. Sadly, she would never get to use it!

In late March of 1947, Margaret became ill. She had a high temperature and a very severe cough. Mum took her to see Doctor Lowe who diagnosed Whooping Cough, and advised Mum to take her straight to Poplar Hospital. Walking from Ellesmere Street to the hospital, Mum was very worried, and when she entered the hospital emergency room, a doctor confirmed the diagnosis. Margaret was admitted into one of the hospital wards and Mum was told to go home. In those days' parents did not stay. It was not the way things were done!

The following morning, Mum returned to the hospital to enquire what was happening and to see her daughter. On entering the Ward, she was approached by a nurse, who asked her who she was there to see? Margaret Patricia Smith, my daughter was her reply. The nurse looked at her, lowered her head and said, "I am so sorry Mrs Smith, but Margaret died last night."

We may look at this in today's light and wonder how such a thing could happen? The facts are things were very different in those days. That is the way things were done. Mum was left to walk back to her home in Ellesmere Street, alone.

The aftermath of Margaret's death was that she was buried, in the coffin of an adult, a stranger unknown to our family, not uncommon for those dark days. Dad returned from the funeral, held at the East London Cemetery, on April 29 1947. He removed the half built dolls pram from his shed, and burned it. As for Mum? She was told by her mother-in-law, who was a kind and lovely person, that she still had two healthy children and to, "put it out of her mind," and just carry on." What impact & effect this had on my poor Mum is unknown, but the advice was accurate; why? Because she had no other choice. At 37 years of age she had survived the bombing and hardships from two world wars, spent two years, as a child working 70 hours per week as a maid, followed by 48 hour weeks, peeling citrus fruit, then forced to bury her only daughter, aged 3 months old.

The celebrated American Playwright, Stephen Adly Guirgis once said, "no parent should ever have to bury a child." How does anyone recover from this? There is no correct answer to this question. In the case of Elsie, my Mum, somehow she just did. I can remember as a very small boy, coming home from school at lunchtime, and after eating, sitting on Mum's lap and listening to the radio. The programme was titled, "Listen with Mother!"

She would sit on her armchair and I would snuggle in, then from the radio came the words I will never forget.

"Are you sitting comfortably? Then I will begin." The reader would then tell a short children's story and as soon as it was finished, I would have to leave the house and run back to school, in order not to be late.

Elsie Daisy Smith, my Mum was an amazing woman, who despite her circumstances, loved and raised us well.

Together with my Dad, she came to Australia in 1976 and together they enjoyed the last years of their lives with their two grandchildren, Dad passing in 1988, then Mum in 1990.

God bless! R.I.P.

Chapter 10.

Spuds, Nitty Norah & the Demon Dentist.

Our little house in Ellesmere Street was built directly opposite a factory. The road was quite narrow, and the factory was still in use in the late 40's, producing tar and ochre products for the shipping industry.

Not as close, but still within, "sniffing range," was a narrow bridge that spanned, "Limehouse Cut," used by barges to travel between the Thames and the River Lee.

The bridge was known as, "Stink House Bridge," the name acquired from the fact that there were no less than three factories, one on each of the four corners of the bridge, all of which produced some of the foulest smelling chemicals known.

Now add to this every home in the district burning coal in the fireplaces, it is easy to see that this was not the cleanest place in the world.

Those of us that lived in houses had a very small garden, and those living in, "The Flats," had none at all.

To supplement food for the family, Dad decided to grow his own vegetables, and the way to do this was to get himself, "an allotment."

Also known as a "Plot," many East-Londoners became "Self-taught Market Gardeners." Our Plot was one of many, situated on the famous, Isle of Dogs.

Directly across the river Thames from Greenwich Great Park, the Isle of Dogs was so named during the reign of Henry the Eighth, in the early 1500's. Henry and his party would rest overnight after hunting Deer, in Greenwich Palace on the south side of the river. His hunting dogs would be taken by boat to the Isle, so that their barking would not keep his majesty awake.

In the late 1800's work began to build Millwall Dock. This was a massive undertaking, and meant excavating thousands of tons of mud. Special machines were built that were to pump the, "foul smelling mud," to a large flat site in the middle of the Isle of Dogs. Originally called the, 'Mud Shoot," but eventually becoming the Mudchute, mud piled up and was left to settle in the hope that the smell would eventually disappear.

In the early 1900's, the Landlord of a local Public House, "The George," still to be found today in Glengall Road, leased a large piece of the mud and developed it to become the home of Millwall Athletic Football Club, however, the smell never quite went away. The Port of London Authority took control and the mudchute was divided into Allotments, one of which was allotted to my Dad.

By the time I had reached the age of ten in 1954, "The Plot," was in full production. The smelly mud had finally settled to become black earth and the smell had finally gone, (or at least I never smelt it). Dad had planted various fruits & vegetables, and come the spring we would start to take them home. Water was limited, so Dad would take old rags, cut them into pieces and dig them into the ground at the end of each season so as to hold water for whatever he planted the following year.

Rhubarb was one of the fruits, and cabbages were a popular vegetable. For a Church Harvest festival I attended in Trinity Church, sometime around 1956, Dad grew a cabbage, that once trimmed weighed in at eight kilograms. The main crop of all was potatoes. Most of the ground was planted with, "Aran Express," which would be harvested in Spring, "Catriona's," in mid-summer and "King Edward," for autumn and stored for winter.

During the main harvest season, Dad, Bob & I would leave Ellesmere Street every Sunday morning for the two mile bike ride. After digging the spuds out, we would put them into hessian sacks, and when it was time to leave, Dad would tie each sack up, with string, leaving a loop for each of us to place over one shoulder, then onto our bikes, past the Port of London Authority Policeman at the gate, and pedal the two miles back home.

By the time we reached the house, the string felt like a knife on my shoulder, the bicycle seat felt like iron and my legs were aching, but we never gave any of this a second thought. It was just life!

Around the same time the London County Council introduced some health services to the East End. Every year, some of the kids at school would get headlice, and sit in class scratching away at their heads. In an attempt to eliminate this, we would all have to go to the school nurse, one class at a time, two times per year.

I can remember standing in line in Susan Lawrence School, slowly inching forward as each kid came out, then when my time came I entered the room, and sitting there waiting to greet me was, "Nitty Nora," which was the nickname that every kid knew her by, because her job was to find headlice, or "Nits," as we called them.

I sat in front of her, and she removed the fine tooth comb from the enamel jug on her desk. The smell of the antiseptic was overwhelming, and with her free hand, she would pull my hair up, then drag the comb through my hair, then after a search of the comb for these "nasty's" she would repeat the process until my entire head had been inspected.

I am glad to report that I was always declared "Nit Free," but I often wondered if she used the same comb for all of us kids????? That antiseptic must have been bloody powerful stuff!

Another, "LCC Children's Health Service," was the dentists. One of these, "kind and gentle," dentist had a clinic in a ground floor flat, in the council estate known as Coventry Cross. This name still brings chills to spine, seventy years later.

It would seem that some public servant, working in the bowels of County Hall in Westminster, had this mental image of kids, running around in the slums of East London, with big, white perfect smiles!!!!! All that was needed was the funding for "Dental Clinics," and a few Dental Nurses. The idea was fine. In practice………..not so fine!

I cannot remember what age I was when Mum took me to my first appointment at Coventry Cross. I remember holding her hand as we crossed Brunswick Rd and seeing the brick built flats, some six stories high. As we walked between the buildings, I was very nervous, scared in fact as this was my first visit ever to a Dentist.

The, Dental Clinic," was in fact just a ground floor apartment, that had a small waiting room and a second room with a dentist chair placed in the middle.

As we walked towards it, I noticed the windows were covered with steel mesh, held in place with a huge padlock, with, "LCC,' clearly stamped on it. Inside the waiting room walls were painted with, 'LCC approved," cream coloured paint. With the exception of a picture of Her Majesty the Queen, the walls were bare.

We sat there, waiting for the nurse to appear, Mum holding my hand, and me quietly panicking. When the nurse came out of the treatment room, my heart hit a new low. She was dressed in a nurse's uniform, a nurse's hat and a black rubber apron that went down to the ground. She was a very large lady, and I did not think she would get through the door, without touching both sides that is.

"NEXT," she yelled as though we were in the next building. Mum & I both rose from our seats and began to walk toward her. "NO PARENTS," she yelled again. Mum sat back down, and I entered alone.

"IN THE CHAIR," she yelled yet again, and quaking in fear, I sat up, trying to be as brave as I could, when the shadow of this huge woman loomed in front of me, no mask, no gloves, just a very loud, "OPEN WIDE," command. To scared not to obey, I opened my mouth as wide as I possibly could.

Now, as I said earlier, I cannot remember my age, but I do remember that I still possessed a couple of my Baby Teeth, one of which was a little loose. As the "Demon Dentist," a name I discovered later, used by the local kids to describe her, groped around in my mouth with a dental mirror and probe, she discovered my loose tooth.

With no warning whatsoever, the dental mirror was pushed under the tooth, and with one quick wrench, (and a nasty laugh from the Demon), my tooth was yanked out of my mouth, and onto the floor, accompanied by the loudest scream I could muster, with this gigantic woman's hands in my mouth!

"YOU"RE FINE,' she said, and led me toward the door, leaving my poor milk tooth on the floor and a cotton swab in my mouth to stem the bleeding.

As I re-entered the waiting room, she pushed me towards Mum and with another, "NEXT" command, it was over. What the public servant from the LCC had in mind, versus what happened to me, were poles apart. I later learned that every kid in the area was petrified of that place and even more so with the Demon Dentist.

Chapter 11.

Shkolnik's, Steamboats & "Souffend."

Getting something, anything that was actually new, was a most unusual thing to happen back in the day. At least it was for most of us kids back then. "Hand-me-downs," was perfectly acceptable, and in fact the most common practice. Toys, schoolbooks, shoes, clothes etc, all handed down from an elder brother or cousin.

I can still see my father examining a pair of short trousers, worn regularly by my brother. "Plenty of wear left in those," he would exclaim and lo & behold, the pants instantly changed ownership, and became mine.

When I needed a coat for school, (we did not have a school uniform in Primary school, but it was expected that short pants and a jacket would be worn), one arrived from my cousins, which although it was obviously too big for me, it was destined to become mine.

I stood in front of Dad, the jacket was placed upon me and the inspection began. First thing I noticed was the elbows, both of which had holes where the material was supposed to be. The arms, severely worn out at the cuff, went past my wrist and covered my hands completely.

"There you are," Dad said looking very pleased with himself. "We'll put patches on the elbows, turn-up the cuffs, and it will be fine." When Mum pointed out that it was, "too big for him," Dad had his reply ready. "He will grow into it!" He was right of course. It took the entire school year, BUT I did grow into it!

All the needs of us kids were satisfied, using the hand-me-down methodology and it worked. Somehow we always had those things we needed, without ever going into a shop to buy them.

Sometime around 1955, Dad was invited to attend a workmates wedding. This was a very big deal for me. It was to be held in a Public House, in Charlton, South London. Dad would be wearing his one, "Sunday Best, suit." Mum would borrow a dress from my Aunt Rose, who still resided at number 50 Ellesmere and worked as a comptometer operator at Unilever House in Blackfriars. Bob was old enough to stay home, which left only me.

As I did not have any, "Sunday Best Clothes," of my own at that time, a call went out to the family, however no one could help, so for the first time in my young life, I was to get a "New Suit," from a real shop.

One week before the wedding, Dad & I left home and headed up Chrisp Street, our local market. I was so excited and still remember it to this day. We passed, "The Toy Bazaar," on our right and "Sussex Bagwash Laundry," on our left, before reaching the corner of Carmen Street. On that corner stood an old two story house, that had somehow survived, when a bomb destroyed the other houses on the block during the war.

Dad & I walked into the house, to find it was now no longer a residence, but in fact a shop. Standing in the half light of what had once been somebody's living room, completely surrounded by clothes, was an old, slightly stooped over gentleman and with a very thick accent, making him hard to understand, he welcomed us inside.

"Welcome to Shkolnik's Tailor Shop," is what I believed I heard him say. By this point, my excitement was completely gone, and I was holding Dads hand as tight as I could. Dad explained that I needed a, "New Suit," to go to a wedding. Mr Scholnick laughed out loud and told us to follow him upstairs, "to the Children's Department."

Dad & I climbed the stairs behind Skolnick. There was very little light, and the smell of mothballs filled the air.

The top front room was indeed the children's area, being filled with clothes racks adorned with boy's jackets and short pants on one side and girls' dresses etc on the other. Skolnick selected a single breasted jacket with matching short pants. I can still see them in my mind's eye, light brown tweed material. I dutifully tried on the jacket and it fit me! No long sleeves, no patches and it had a label pinned to it with the price. "£1.5 shillings." The pants were held up to my front, and it was determined they would fit. I was about to become the owner of my first new suit.

Dad sent me downstairs to wait for him as I was deemed too young to witness the bartering that would take place. After a few minutes, Dad joined me, carrying a brown paper parcel, held together with string. It was time to celebrate, because I now had a new suit to go to my first wedding.

It was some years later that I came to realise that Skolnick's Tailor shop, was not that at all. It was a "second-hand clothing," shop and my new suit was not new at all; however I did not care in the slightest. I wore my suit to the wedding, and I wore it with pride. It was mine, "bought & paid for," simply brilliant!

Buying a suit like this was not easy for my family. Money was very tight, and this was clearly a "luxury item," and they were few and far between. Despite this, Mum & Dad did all they could to see us kids had some fun. We always had a holiday, every year, usually for a week in a caravan on the coast. Clacton-on-Sea, Littlehampton, Canvey Island were among some of the places we went. Mum, Bob & I and usually Dad, however there were a number of times he would take us to the caravan site and get us all booked in, then on Sunday afternoon he would leave for home, work all week then return the following Saturday to take us home. He simply could not afford for all of us to go, but made sure we kids got our holiday.

Another place that was always popular with EastEnders's can be found at the wide estuary of the Thames River, that place being, Southend-on-Sea. It is close enough for a day trip, which we did on more than one occasion.

Southend-on-Sea, or "Souffend," as we called it had everything a Cockney kid could want. Dodgem Cars, Racer's, Haunted House, plus stalls where you could win all sorts of prizes, provided, of course you had the money to spend. All along, "The Front," or Marine Parade there was Arcades, full of slot machines, and rides. Most of the machines took a Penny Coin, thus the name, "Penny Arcades."

Further along, but still close enough to walk was, "The Kursaal." An amazing mix of booths, arcades, swings, merry-go-rounds, you name it!

If I am correct, the famous English actress, Dame Helen Mirren, worked as a sideshow assistant in the Kursaal, whilst growing up in Westcliff-on-Sea. (Her mother was also an East Ender, although she was born in Chiswick on the south side of the River Thames.

I only ever got to go to the Kursaal on one occasion, when my Aunt Rose gave me sixpence, to take with me on the one-day-return train trip, when I was around 8 years old.

On this occasion, we went to Stepney East Railway Station on Commercial Road, known today as Limehouse DLR Station.

In those days, it was a British rail Station, and the trains ran from Fenchurch Street in the City to Southend Central. Every Cockney, Post-War kid knew about the, "Train to Souffend!" It was one of the great treats of its time and lingers in my memory more than six decades later.

We would walk from Ellesmere Street until we reached the station, then climb the stairs up to the, "Eastbound Platform," and stand as close as possible to the edge, waiting for those tell-tale-signs to arrive. Sometimes the sound of the wheels on the tracks was first, but usually it was the unique sounds and sights, that only a Steam train can make. As it approached the station, the driver would blow the whistle, and a burst of steam would burst out of the top of boiler. The smoke from the chimney was black and as the engine passed us, we could see the driver, his hand on the controls, the engineer shovelling coal in the fire. What could possibly be more exciting to an eight year old boy than this huge, dirty, noisy, wonderful machine.

As soon as it came to a stop, we would run for the Second Class Carriage and hopefully find an empty carriage. There were no corridors on the train in those days, so each compartment had its own door, with seats each side, and a netting material racks above.

Once aboard, the first thing to do was to grab the leather strap that was hanging out of the inside of the door, pull hard and release it causing the window to drop down, then us kids would put our heads out of the window and as the train slowly moved away, the smoke would billow out of the chimney, the steam would come up from the pistons, the noise would be deafening, and we were on our way. Southend-on-Sea was a mere 35 miles away. As we passed factories and houses, the train gathered speed, however the best was yet to come.

Following the Thames Valley meant there were very few hills. Not really any gradients to speak of, but there was one tunnel to go through and we were ready. As the train went in, we stuck our heads out, Dad yelling for us to keep our eyes closed, so as not to get a, "Cinder," basically hot black soot from the coal, in our eyes. The smell of the coal burning, the steam rising, and the sound was simply the best. If we were really lucky, the driver would blow the steam whistle, just as the train emerged back into the light. Absolutely delighted with the experience, we would pull our head from the window, open our eyes, and show Dad the biggest smiles, after which he would take his handkerchief out of his pocket, spit on it, and Bob & I would get the black rings of soot, "washed," form our faces, ready to arrive at Southend Central Station, walk down Pier Hill and hopefully get an "Ice Cream Cornet," from "Rossi's Soft Ice Cream Van," before crossing Marine parade and taking in the wonderful sights and sounds of the funfair known as, "Adventure Land."

Another unique and for us kids, wondrous attraction in Souffend was the Southend-on-Sea Pier.

Almost every seaside town in England has a Pier, however the Southend Pier had a claim to fame, that no others could copy. With a total length of 1.33 miles, or 2158 metres, it was, (and I believe still is), the longest pleasure pier in the world. Running out from the shoreline into the Thames Estuary, its iron piles are firmly anchored into the mud which can clearly be seen at low tide. When it opened in the early 1890's it was the first pier to have Pier Railway.

I am unsure as to when the following event took place. I know I was quite young, maybe 5 or 6, Mum, Bob & I took a trip to Southend, only this time we did not go on the Steam Train. Instead we took the bus to Aldgate, walked down The Minories, past the Tower of London, to Tower Pier. There waiting for all of the passengers to board, us included tied up to the pier, flags flying in the wind stood a magnificent sight: The Royal Sovereign.

Built in Scotland in 1948 she was still very new and her white hull, two masts and one funnel, she was a sight to behold.

Once onboard, she drifted out into the River Thames. The ships horn blew as a request for the engineers on shore to open the two leaves of Tower Bridge.

Passing under this great bridge was an unbelievable experience. Dad had told me, the evening before this trip that my Grandad was a, "Rivet Boy," and helped to build the bridge in the late 1800's.

Butler & Colonial Wharf to our right and St Katherines Dock to our left, we were on our way.

We saw all the landmarks as we sailed east. The 400 year old infamous tavern, "The Prospect of Whitby," and a second Public House, built in the 1500's, "The Grapes, in Narrow St, where Charles Dickens wrote some of his famous novels. Greenwich Park, where the 24 hour clock for Greenwich Meantime is located, with the Isle of Dogs opposite, showing where the Steamship, "The Great Eastern," was built & launched.

For a couple of Cockney kids, this trip was simply brilliant, with something to surprise us around every bend in the river. Arriving at Southend, we disembarked the Sovereign and she continued her voyage to Margate and Ramsgate, with the promise of being back at the pierhead at 3.00pm, for the voyage home.

The pierhead itself, like the rest of Southend, had a funfair, including dodgem cars. There was also a Royal Naval Lifeboat Station there, complete with rescue boats. We boarded one of the trains and travelled the length of the pier, before getting off and of course heading straight for Rossi's, the best Ice Cream in the World!

Our short stay in Southend was great fun. We not only got to go on some of the funfair rides, we even had fish & chips for our lunch. There was no greater fun anywhere, especially for a Cockney kid. As time passed, we began to walk back to the pier, passing the backs of the famous Southend Beach Huts, all placed facing the water, with a small gap between each one. Used by both owners and "renter's," for changing into their swimwear and enjoying their lunch etc, they are now long gone.

Brother Bob decided that it was good fun to run between the huts, hide for a while then reappear from between two different huts, usually in front of Mum & I, accompanied by a loud, "Boo!" This went on for a while, until, Bob disappeared, the same as before, but did not reappear at all. Mum seized my hand, and started to call Bobs name, softly at first then louder and louder. He voice echoed through the gaps between the huts, but Bob did not reappear. Mum & I went up & down the back of the Beach Huts, then along the fronts, asking people if they had seen him, but, to no avail. He was gone!

Mum decided to enlist the assistance of one of Southend-on-Sea's finest. In those days there were policeman on the streets and they were helpful. The search officially begun, although finding a small boy, in a very crowded Southend was never going to be easy.

Mum & I waited at the entrance to the pier, after all if Bob was simply missing, surely he would head for the pier? Looking out towards the pierhead, we saw the M.V. Royal Sovereign in the distance, as she slowly made her return from the Channel Ports and back into the Estuary. Still no sign of Bob, despite half of the Policemen in the town searching for him.

Our fellow passengers streamed past us as we stood by the pier ticket office, all heading for the same boat, and we watched the little pier trains taking them all out, but we could not join them, at least not yet.

After waiting for what felt like an eternity, Bob suddenly arrived. There were no Police Officers with him. He just arrived alone, but he had something with him which puzzled me. Mum was both relieved and angry, because she had her eldest boy back, completely unharmed. He stood there, looking as innocent as possible and sucking on a, "Rossi's Soft Ice Cream Cornet,"

We immediately run up the stairs that led to the pier train platform, only to see the majestic sight of the Sovereign sailing away from the pierhead on her way back to London…………..without us!

My dear Mother was a soft-spoken lady. I had never seen her raise her voice in anger, however she surely did on that day, using words my young ears had never heard before!

We made the trudge up Pier Hill, and then on to Southend Central Station, to get the train back to Stepney East. It was fortunate that Mum had enough money for the tickets, which once purchased, we boarded the train for home, in third class, of course.

Now there were no mobile phones in the middle of the Twentieth Century. No internet, no Facebook, no Messenger! No way in fact, for Mum to let Dad know of our circumstances.

Now as things would happen, after completing a full day's deliveries, Dad parked his lorry in the yard of Chas. Poulter, and the weather being fine, he made the decision to walk to Tower Pier and meet the Royal Sovereign on her return. Upon her arrival, he waited eagerly for his family to walk down the gangplank, but can you imagine what was going through his mind when we failed to appear?

He was eventually informed that the said missing Smith family trio, failed to re-board at Southend.

By the time he walked back to Ellesmere Street, Bob & I were in bed, however that did not stop Dad from coming up and, "reading-the-riot-act," to Bob, whilst I hid under the bed covers to avoid any involvement.

It was a very long time after this, before Rossi's Soft Serve Ice Cream was ever mentioned again in our house!

Chapter 12.

School Milk & Ration Books.

My first day of school was in the very old building that stood one block away from my little home at 46 Ellesmere St. It was called Alton Street school in those days, but later changed to St. Saviours. Sometime in 1950/1 us kids were told to put all the contents from our desk, into a small cardboard box we found waiting for us. I remember my box was blue, with my name and class number clearly written on the side. We then put on our coats, and followed our teacher, out of the school, across Alton Street, then followed Kirby Street towards the brand new school, "Susan Lawrence (JM) Primary School, in Cordelia Street.
Each one of us walked with our, "buddy," or partner, carrying our desk contents, diligently following our teacher, until we walked into this brand new building and into our classroom. I still remember the smell of paint, and the newness of it all.
This was to be my daily ritual, until I moved on to high school.

Mrs Henry was my teacher. A rather large lady, always well dressed in clothes that covered her from neck to toe. The first words ever written on the brand new blackboard at the front of the class was, "Welcome to Susan Lawrence School."

Sometime around 10.15 or so, we went outside for what is called recess today. We knew it as Playtime, and was at that time we were given our, "School Milk." It consisted of a small bottle, (one third of a pint from memory), with a silver foil cap, which we would remove to insert the straw supplied, and drink, prior to going into the playground. School milk was available, every school day when I went to this school, and remained that way until 1971, when the then Secretary of State for Education, one Margaret Thatcher stopped the supply for all children over the age of seven. She was aptly named, "Thatcher Thatcher Milk Snatcher." My dear old Mum was disgusted at this and never forgave her for it!

Warm milk in Summer & cold, (sometimes frozen) milk in winter was a big part of life for post-war kids, as was having to use, "Ration Books," on trips to the market with Mum. Chrisp Street market was a street market, with most of the stalls at the south end, this was until the new Chrisp Street market opened, at about the same time as the school. I used to love going shopping with Mum when I was small, walking up Chrisp St, past the Guilford Arms, which stood on the corner of Godalming Rd. I remember Mum told me about one trip to the market, sometime before I was born. She had my brother in a pram and just as she began her walk back towards home, she heard a sound that she was well used to……..Air Raid Siren. The slow rise and fall of that siren sent shivers through the spine of every East-

Ender and Mum was no exception. She knew she had a short window of time until she could get to shelter, in Westhorp's factory.

She quickly picked up her pace, heading for home & the relevant safety of Westhorp's, but as she crossed over Godalming Road, a bomb fell on the houses diagonally opposite where she was standing. She threw herself over the pram in an effort to protect her son, and as she did, the large lead-glass window that was the pride of the, "Saloon Bar," at the Guilford Arms, was blown out of the wall, where it had stood for years and, according to Mum, flew horizontally for about 5 or 6 feet, still in one piece, before falling to the ground and smashing into thousands of small pieces.

She quickly crossed the road, and made her way to the shelter in Westhorp's, all in one piece. It was the second time she had been caught outside during the bombing, somehow managing to escape both completely unscathed. Years later she would proudly tell the story of how she was the very last person to see the Guilford Arms Saloon Bar window in one piece!

Thankfully there were no bombs or flying windows as Mum & I walked to the newly opened Chrisp Street market.

What had been a street market for more than 100years, and seriously damaged as a result of the blitz, had been replaced, as part of the Lansbury Estate. Chrisp Street Market boasted a Clock Tower, Market Stalls, Covered Arcade Shops, Two Public Houses, (The Festival Inn & The Festive Briton), plus a number of larger shops.

My favourite shop, as a small child was, "The Co-Op!"
Co-op was an abbreviation of, "The Co-operative Group,
formed by a group of men, in Rochdale, with the first shop
in Toad Lane, 100 years before I was born and by
coincidence, about one mile from place where I was
evacuated during the war. The intention was to supply
basic staple foods to working class people, at a fair price.
Any profits were paid back to the shoppers themselves, as
a, "Dividend," or "divi," as most people referred to it.
My earliest memories of this was walking into the Co-op in
Chrisp Street, which was made up of two shops, side-by-
side. On the left was the grocery section, but my favourite
was next door, The Co-op butchers. I can still see, "Jack,"
the butcher, standing behind the counter with his blue &
white apron. He would always say hello to me, and give me
a demonstration of his Knife-sharpening-skills, slashing his
butchers knife up & down on the sharpening steel.
Mum would order our meat, however for the first nine years
following the end of WW2, food rationing was still in place.
Later on, after rationing was lifted and we could buy beef
from Argentina & Uruguay, Lamb from New Zealand &
Bacon from Denmark, our diet improved immensely, but
before this a, "Ration Stamp, was required. The limits were
very low:

- Bacon.   4 oz's
- Sugar.   8 oz's
- Tea.   2 oz's
- Cheese.   2 oz's (5 oz's for verge's).
- Butter   2 oz's

Meat was rationed by price. This meant a maximum spend, per week, (rationing was on a weekly basis), of 1 shilling and two pence, (approximately £4.00 in 2020).

Mum's choice was usually mincemeat, simply because it was the cheapest, therefore she got more.

I was always given the task of handing over the ration book stamps, the money and telling Jack ,Mum's, "divi number."...........395570..........still remember it after more than 70 years!

Chapter 13.

Coronation and Tarry Blocks.

1952 was a big year in Poplar, in fact it was a big year everywhere in the UK and British Commonwealth. February 6 of that year saw the death of King George VI. Albert Frederick Arthur George was known as, "Bertie," to his friends, ascended to the throne on December 11, 1936, when his elder brother, King Edward VIII, abdicated the throne in order for him to marry an American divorcee, Wallace Simpson.

It was heavily rumoured at the time, that he did not want to be King, but had little choice in the matter. Possessing a bad stammer, he hated public speaking, but with the help of an Australian speech specialist, one Lionel Logue, he improved greatly. Following his death, he was succeeded by his eldest daughter, Queen Elizabeth II.

Being at the tender age of 8 at that time, I admit that none of this had any real significance. To me it was business as usual, however in June 1953, things changed dramatically. June 2, 1953 was announced as the official date for the Coronation of Queen Elizabeth II. What was far more important, was that the announcement included, "street parties to celebrate."

It was eight short years since the war had ended and Poplar was in the early stages of trying to recover. The London County Council, "Slum Clearance Act," was in full swing. Bomb damaged buildings had been mostly cleared with new structures rising out of the ashes, including Chrisp Street market with its Clocktower, two new pubs, The Festive Briton and the Festival Inn plus new flats, maisonettes and high rise accommodation.

Ration books had finally been phased-out and new varieties of foods were appearing in the shops.

In addition to all of these exciting events, a new and wondrous technology was about to hit.....Television!

Now as exciting as this was, for us kids in Poplar, it was still a dream, a mystery that we had heard about, but were yet to see.

I remember walking from our house in Ellesmere Street, sometime in the 50's to the new Aberfeldy Estate. In one of the new shops that had been built, they sold Television's. When we arrived, we were met by the sight of dozens of people, all standing outside the shop, desperately trying to see past the people in front of them. Georgie Smith, (my mate from Godalming Rd) and I joined the crowd and slowly eased closer to the window, and lo & behold there it was! Sitting on a small table and almost touching the glass on the inside of the window, was a 14 inch screen, black & white television. The name, "Cossor," was written in gold letters immediately below the screen. The picture on the screen was of a little girl in the middle of a circle, surrounded by white lines and squares. At the bottom of the screen were the letters, "BBC."

We were mesmerised at the sight of this marvel, and sat there staring for ages, however I remember the thought going through my head, "Why does it look like it is snowing?"

Snow or no-snow, Television had arrived and us kids were both delighted & amazed by the wonder of it!

It would be a long time before we had our own TV, however our bus-driver neighbour, Mr Freeman, (you may remember him for the Christmas morning chimney fire), had purchased one in the early days of 1953 and it stood proudly in his front room. It was on this magnificent, "black & white TV," on June 2, 1953, some 20 or so people crammed into that little room to watch the Coronation of Her Majesty the Queen.

I can still remember sitting in front of this little brown box, with its eight inch screen, looking at the Royal Coach, heading towards Westminster. Everything seemed to have a green tinge to it. I found out later that this was caused by a special screen, placed in front of the TV, to "eliminate the snowy effects on the screen."

The, "rabbit ears," aerial was sitting on top of the box, and was occasionally adjusted, to improve the picture, although I confess I could see no change at all. After a short while, we had to leave in order for the next group of neighbours to see this modern wonder.

Outside of the house was a hive of activity. The street party was being prepared, with everyone bringing their chairs, tables, crockery cutlery etc, and constructing the longest table I had ever seen, right down the middle of Ellesmere Street! At 3.00pm sharp the party began. Sandwiches, orange cordial drinks for the kids, tea for the adults. The bunting was strung across the road, and British flags were everywhere to be seen.

The memory of that great day is indelibly stamped into my mind. It was a day for us Cockneys to enjoy, knowing that despite the most intense bombing in history, we were back. The Queen was on her throne, and England was getting on her feet again.

Life in Poplar in the fifties had its good times. Sadly it also had its, not-so-good times. People were resilient and they kept a strong sense of optimism, even when things got tough. I can remember having a bowl of bread & milk for dinner on more than one occasion. I didn't care of course, but poor old Mum must have been worried to death, not knowing what each new day would bring?

Keeping warm in winter was also a struggle. Coal was in short supply and expensive, but it wasn't the only thing that burned!!!

Some 100 or so years before WWII, around 1839, traffic noise became a major problem on the streets of London. Haulage carts, just like the one's still in use by Henry Green & Co. in the fifties', had metal rims, as did the Handsome Cabs, and just about every horse-drawn vehicle of the day. The granite cobblestones that had been used to build London's streets, were both hard & durable for these steel rims. The problem was that they were also extremely noisy, bringing complaints from all quarters of business & commerce.

The solution to this problem was to replace the hard stones with wooden blocks. Over the course of approximately 60 years, hard wooden blocks replaced granite, with Threadneedle Street & Regent Street being two of the famous streets to make this change.

Wood was imported from all over the world for use in this type of road building, much of it from Canada and Australia. Jarrah was the most preferred wood and it was imported into England from Australia. It was the hardest of the woods available and as such, it lasted longer, and it also absorbed less, "horse urine," thus reducing the putrid stink on London's famous thoroughfares!

To protect these wooden blocks from the harsh steel wheels of the heavy horse & carts, a new product was used, that being Tarmacadam. This was used to cover the wooden blocks in the early 1800's, but the steel wheels would leave, "deep ruts," in the surface. That was until an entrepreneuring young man, operating his business, "Cassell's Patent Lava Stone Works," in the Eastend suburb of Millwall, John Henry Cassell patented, "Lava Stone."

By spreading tar, sand & gravel over the wooden blocks, then compacting the mixture, "Tarry Blocks," as we Cockney's referred to them were used across London & beyond. And it did not go unnoticed by the resourceful people of Poplar.

According to various reports, this highly inflammable material was recognised as a commodity of value by another entrepreneur, none other than the now famous billionaire, Lord Alan Sugar.

Born Alan Michael Sugar in Hackney, East London in 1947, he was raised in a Council flat, and attended a local school. Assuming the reports to be true, it seems Lord Sugar witnessed some of the roads in his local area having the old wooden blocks removed, ready for new materials and he quickly realised they were worth money as fuel for the locals.

The story goes that the workers who were removing the old, "Tarry Blocks," informed him that they burned brilliantly. He collected them, cut them into bundles of sticks, "and flogged, (sold) them. The rest, as they say, is history.

For me, Kerby Street was where our source of heat came from. The sight of a whole bunch of locals picking up as many blocks as they could manage still lingers in my mind. One family filled a baby's pram until it was over-flowing. At this time, my dad had purchased a second-hand Austin A35 van, and it too was used to collect the precious blocks.

I well remember Mum being very annoyed after a trip in the van to Clacton-on-Sea. It seems that her sister, my Aunt Milly and brother-in-law accompanied them, and on arrival in Clacton, Milly complained that her backside was very uncomfortable. Dad had thrown the old bus seat back into the van without checking to ensure that all the blocks had been removed. Aunt Milly had ridden the sixty or so miles from Chingford to Clacton with a large, (and very lumpy) tarry block , "sticking-up-her-arse," as the old man had eloquently said it. As I said, Mum was not amused.

Every kid who grew up in the east end at that time, will have memories of sitting in front of a roaring fire in the middle of a cold winter, mesmerised by the flames and the heat. The problem with using old pieces of a wooden street for fuel, is that once the blocks were heated, the tar would melt and the sand, and gravel would fly out of the fire, like red-hot projectiles, usually accompanied by a loud cracking noise.

If you never grabbed the shovel from the hearth and run to pick-up the hot missile, before it burnt a hole in the rug, you probably did not grow up in east London in the fifties'??

Chapter 14.

Bikes and burnt bums.

There was 42 kids in my class at Susan Lawrence and in our last year we had a teacher who made a huge impression on all of us. An amazing man by the name of Herbert Enever.

Mr Enever was old school, (no pun intended). He had been in the army during the war, then in India, before being demobbed and becoming a teacher. Nothing was ever to much trouble for him. He taught everything from the three R's to sport and country dancing.

He stood around 6 ft 4 inches, (195 cm's), but very thin, so too us kid's he was a giant. He had the biggest hands I ever saw, and if you were not behaving as you should in his classroom, he would use his index finger like a, "policeman's cosh," tapping heavily on the top of your head, whilst at the same time he would tell you what you had dome wrong, each word accompanied by a, "tap," on the head.

Mr Enever trained the football team in winter, the cricket team in summer, always being wherever the games were played on Saturday mornings. He took our class to Poplar Baths every week, and it was him who taught me to swim.

I remember two boys fighting in the playground one day. Mr Enever pulled them apart, then at lunchtime, he put up the boxing ring in the school hall, put 15oz. boxing gloves on each of the two boys, and they would be made to, "fight it out." Of course, with such large gloves it was impossible for either of them to be hurt, and when Mr Enever told them to stop, they would be made to shake hands and it was all over.

He was a dedicated and great teacher who had a big influence on my life. Real old school!

When I was 18 and working as an apprentice electrician, I went back to Susan Lawrence, met Mr Enever and took him to a pub in Chrisp street market, The Festive Britain, and together we enjoyed a couple of beers. A memory I still cherish to this day.

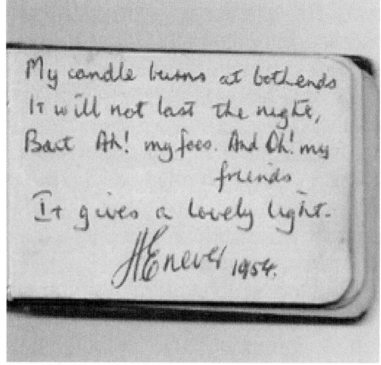

My candle burns at both ends
It will not last the night,
But Ah! my foes. And Oh! my
friends
It gives a lovely light.

HEnever 1954.

"Mr Enever," in my autograph book!

It during my last year at primary school that I got my first two wheeler bike. When Dad told me about this, I had visions of going to Roberts, the bike shop in East India Dock road, and picking out a new, bright & shiny bike. I should have known better. Dad was a third generation Cockney. He would not dream of, "wasting money," going to a shop. Not when there were plenty of bargains to be had in the Sunday markets.

Not too far from Poplar, in the direction of the City, East Londoners had the choice of two Sunday markets. Petticoat Lane was in Middlesex Street, just outside of the City of

London. This was the place for clothing, especially for ladies, crockery, hats, footwear etc. An open street market, with stalls both side of the road, it was always a fun place to visit. Coffee shops & stalls, Jewish bakeries selling kosher foods & salt beef rolls were all part of the day's enjoyment. And of course, the Cockney's favourite, purchased in a china bowl from Tubby Isaac's stall, covered in vinegar before devouring. "Jellied Eels!"

The other Sunday market was not as famous and nowhere near as glamorous as Petticoat Lane, Club Row was the place for puppies, kittens, chickens, racing pigeons and the like! Second-hand tools were another popular commodity, and on a vacant piece of land in the middle of Club Row, there could be found bikes!

Well, not exactly bikes. A more accurate description would be, "bits of bikes." Spread out on the ground were all the parts needed to build a bike. This is where Dad & I went one Sunday morning, taking the bus to Aldgate, then walking the rest of the way. The first thing was the frame, then once that was secured, wheels, handlebars, saddle, cranks, bike chain, etc, etc. It may be hard to understand how all of this happened, but I assure you it did. Not only did we buy most of the things required, we took them all home on the bus, I never saw anything untoward in this, after all, didn't everyone we knew do the same thing? Every day after school, the bike parts came out of the shed, and when dad arrived home we would work on putting all the parts together. The final result was a black framed, 24 inch wheeled bike, with straight handlebars and a, "Brooks," leather saddle. No gears, but cable brakes with brand new, (the only part that was new), brake blocks.

Shortly after my eleventh birthday, in 1955 I joined my brother Bob and one other friend, for a Sunday bike ride. No self-respecting Cockney boy could hold his head up in Poplar, unless he had completed his Sunday bike ride.

There were two destinations recognised as suitable by other boys in the district. The most popular was Southend-on-Sea, thirty five miles to the east. It was a relatively flat trip, with only one small climb, (known as Bread-n-Cheese Hill). A return trip of 70 miles, or 112 kilometres.

The other destination was Paddock Wood, a hop-growing village in the beautiful county of Kent.

This was the destination chosen for me.

Similar in distance from Poplar as Southend, Paddock Wood presented a few more challenges. Firstly it was south, which meant it was on the opposite side of the River Thames. Second, Kent is very hilly, meaning we had to climb a number of hills, including the infamous Wrotham Hill, and of course, descend those same hills on our return journey.

Looking back on this journey it is difficult to imagine a number of things……..why did our parents allow us to do this? How dangerous was it? How did a 24 inch wheel bike, with no gears, pedalled by a scrawny eleven year old kid get there and back?

I don't know the answer to any of these questions, but what I do know is that we did this and thought nothing of it. It was just something kids do!!!!! Can you imagine anything like this today????? The mind boggles.

That, "Home-Made-Bike," opened up a whole new world for me. The world, (or at least beyond Poplar) was my oyster. I could go anywhere. And I did.

One of our favourite, "rides," was Greenwich park. Up Chrisp Street, cross over East India Dock Rd, Cotton Street, Prestons Rd, around the walls, (Dock walls both sides of the rd.), over the swing bridge, then the lift-up bridge, finally the Island gardens.

It was there we entered the lift that descended down and into the Greenwich Foot Tunnel, then riding through the narrow tunnel that run beneath the River Thames and riding the lift up the other side, through the village and into Greenwich park

The Royal Observatory Greenwich, designed by Sir Christopher Wren, (the same architect that designed St Mary-le-Bow and St Pauls Cathedral) and opened in, 1676 stands in Greenwich Park and was always the first place for us to visit. It was an amazing place for us kids. On display was the 24 Hour Clock, sitting in the stone wall that surrounded the old building, its huge face was like a magnet. Immediately below it on the ground was a yellow line with the words, "Greenwich Meridian," the imaginary line that went from Greenwich, through both the North & South Poles, and ended back where it started. The line of longitude, 0 degrees, that divided the world East – West, just as the Equator divides the North – South. We would stand on the line, pretend we were in both east & west at the same time, and look at the clock showing Greenwich Meantime.

There is also a statue in Greenwich Park, built on the top of a hill, looking down on the Old Royal Naval College that stands on the south bank of the Thames.

General Wolfe, was born in Kent, lived in Greenwich, and is famous for his victory in 1759, when he sailed up the Saint Lawrence River in Canada, broke the French siege and took the City of Quebec, thus securing Canada for the British. He is buried in St Alfeges church, also in Greenwich.

Us kids would stand in front of the statue, and look across the river to the Isle of Dogs, so named in the reign of King Henry VIII. The story goes that Henry would come down the river from Westminster in order to hunt deer in Greenwich. The Palace of Placentia stood on the Southbank of the river, (where the Old Royal Naval College stands today) and he would both entertain and sleep there. The Royal Hunting Hounds that accompanied him were excellent hunters. They were also excellent at barking all night, so in order for Henry to sleep, the dogs were taken across the river by boat, and kept far enough away, so as not to disturb His Majesty's slumbers.

When it was time for us to make the return ride home, we would sit on our bikes in front of General Wolfe, look around to see if we were being watched by a Park Keeper, ("Parkie," to us kid's), then if it was all clear, we ride down the grassy hill in front of the statue, as fast as we could and head for the foot-tunnel.

Like most boys, one of the things we always wanted to do was to, "Go Fishing." In Poplar this meant only one thing, The Regents Canal.

Part of the great Canal systems that covered England The Regents Canal was opened in 1820, linking the Grand Union Canal in Paddington, to Limehouse Basin & the River Thames.

Eight and a half miles, (13.8 km's) in length, it meanders through West London, including. "Little Venice," in Paddington, following the northern perimeter of Regents Park, Camden Lock, through North London, and then passing Victoria Park.

Once again the bike played an important part of our lives. With the fishing rod strapped to the crossbar, we would ride the two miles, stopping at, "The Tackle Shop," on Grove Road to buy maggots for bait, we would head for Sewardstone Road, and Piggott House.

The canal had a towpath on the Park side; however it was fenced off to the public in those days. The locked gate to the towpath meant us kids could not use it. The fish in the canal had been regularly stocked, by an illustrious group known as the, London Angling Association, or LAA for short. Their members had keys to the gate, and they would set up on the towpath with their fancy fishing rods, expensive equipment, and seats with umbrella's attached, to keep off the rain. Definitely, "out-of-bounds," for us kid's, or "scruffy little urchins," as one of them once referred to me!

We didn't care at all. At the back of Pigott House, an old brick council-owned block of flats, was a six foot steel fence, behind which was a narrow dirt strip, which formed part of the canal bank. Right in front of that bank, was a deep hole in the canal, and the fish loved it.

We chose that place for two reasons. One was the deep hole and the other was a very large, (but very easy to climb), Horse Chestnut Tree, which was right alongside the fence. So leaving the bike on one side, it was over the fence for us, threading live maggots on to the hook and then waiting for that float to go under. We would catch Roach & Perch, often in large numbers, much to the disgust of the LAA anglers on the other bank.

In the summer of 1956, my Dad organised a job for me. We had six weeks holidays from school, and I was to spend the first four of them working in Millwall Docks.

To say that I was excited at the prospect would have been an understatement, however I was still very nervous. I had not been into the Docks since Dad took me as a youngster, but every kid around wanted to work there. Almost all of the Dad's worked there and most kids expected to follow in their footsteps, so I was really envied by my mates. I couldn't wait for the day to come when I would become, (even if only for a short time), "A London Dockie."

On that first day, I got up with Dad, and had breakfast, then Dad got his bike and I got mine and off we went.

I followed behind Dad, down Upper North Street, over East India Dock Rd, past Pennyfields, (too early in the morning for any Chinese to be around), then into the Docks, passing through those gates at the bottom of West India Dock Road and past The PLA Policeman and into the hustle & bustle. As we crossed the train lines that were half-hidden between the cobblestones, Dad yelled a warning back to me. "Be careful not to get your front wheel into the train tracks, or you know what will happen!" I knew very well what would happen. Poor old Dad was riding his trusty bike home from the Docks one day. It seems that the Russian ship he was helping to unload, had a very hospitable Captain. In thanks for unloading the ship in quick time, he had given Dad a bottle of Vodka. Now if Dad had tried to pass through the gates with Vodka in his possession, he would be arrested, charged and most likely fired from his job. But as he once told me, "You can bring Vodka through the gates, right past the PLA Policeman, provided it was inside of you." Apparently Dad had consumed enough of this spirit to impair his eyesight and impact his sense of balance. By now you can see where this is leading and you be correct. Dad forgot about the train lines; his front wheel did indeed get caught in them. The bike came to an abrupt stop but unfortunately dad did not. He was launched over the handlebars, and after a very short flight, he made a very unsophisticated three-point-landing on the unforgiving granite block road. This three-point-landing consisted of his two knees, which as a result were left with very little skin left upon them and the third point of landing being his nose, which also lost most of its skin, plus under the large swelling, the bone was broken.

The Vodka must have been doing its job well because despite all of his injuries, he still rode his bike home, (and to this day I have no idea how).

Taking care not to repeat Dad's acrobatic antics, I rode into Millwall Dock and as instructed, reported to the Gear shed and a very large man, known to all as, "Iron-Chest-Harry." The Gear Shed was exactly that, a shed, made from timber, green in colour but desperately in need of a coat of paint.

As I opened the door and went inside, the smell of Jute filled the air. It was strong, pungent, but, at least to me, was quite pleasant. It was a smell I would get used to over the next month.

Iron Chest Harry was sitting in his chair, mug of tea in hand. I recognised him immediately from the description given to me by my Dad. Harry stood close to two meters in height, and towered over me as he stood up to greet me. But his height was not the reason for his nickname. Harry never wore a shirt. It was July when I met him in the Gear Shed, summer, so the weather was warm. Harry was wearing a white singlet. His muscles were huge and I made a mental note to never upset him. Summer or Winter whatever the weather, Iron Chest Harry wore his singlet. I never asked why???

The Gear Shed was full of ropes, (thus the smell of Jute). Harry explained to me what my job would be.

In 1959 the London Docks were still in full swing. The days of Containers were looming but loading and unloading ships was still performed in the same manner that it had been for well over 100 years. When the great Tea Clippers of the 1800's, The Cutty Sark being one of the fastest of her time, carried Tea in wooden tea chests from India, they would be unloaded by Stevedore's, men using steam driven cranes and ropes. Rope slings, rope nets, etc. and there in the Gear Shed covering the walls and floor, were all of those ropes still used at that time.

Stevedore's were paid by the hour, most of them casuals, picked to work only when the ships came into the Dock. The ships Captains wanted their loads removed as quickly as possible, loaded with whatever they were to leave port with, and back to sea. Stevedore's were paid a bonus if they completed these tasks in the time frame allowed. Speed was the number one driver.

Safety was a poor second in those days and many accidents happened, some of them fatal. The common cause for this was, "Gear failure." Rope slings and nets wear with use. Wear equates to weakness and if not found in time, that weakness will results in breakage. If a rope sling breaks as it is hanging from the hook of a crane, whatever is in that sling drops. Those Stevedore's standing underneath, ready to unload it, had seconds to escape. Sadly, many did not.

Harry explained to me that my job was to check every sling, every net for weak spots. I was to sit on an upturned half-barrel, take each sling or net, pass the rope slowly through my hands, looking for damage.

Once a suspect area was found, I would twist the rope in the opposite direction to which it was made. This would open the strands. Holding on tight to each side of the rope,

I would turn my hands like the crank on a bicycle as hard as I could. If the strands showed signs of wear and the jute strands were frayed, that sling was no longer fit to be used. I spent the best part of that 4 weeks performing this task. If a sling with damage went out for use, men could be seriously injured, or worse. I had a heavy responsibility for a 15 year old with a temporary job!

One day while I was sitting on my barrel, running ropes through my hands, Iron Chest harry came in, looked at me and said, "come on Son, we have a job to do on one of the ships." We proceeded to load up a wheelbarrow with rope and other things selected by Harry and we made our way down the dock. As we walked harry explained that one of the ships was being loaded with copper ingots, an expensive cargo and they were loading, "over the bow of the ship," which meant that as the crane swung each pallet of copper from the dock to the Ship, it had to travel over the gap between the dock and the ship. Our job was to hang a cargo net over the bow of the ship, then secure the other side to the dock so that in the event of anything falling, it would not be lost in the water below. I had been a boy scout since the age of eleven and knew how to tie knots. Harry was very impressed.

It was walking back to the Gear Shed that I first saw London Dock Lavatories! They were like no others I had ever seen before. Let me explain.

First was a long half-pipe or large gutter approximately 18 inches, (45 cm.) high and the same in depth. It ran for a length of about 20 feet, (6 meters) along the edge of the waterside. A large pump supplied water from the dock into the half-pipe so that it flowed constantly through and out into the dock at the other end. Built over this mini-river was a series of seats, toilet style seats, with a hole in the middle directly over the flowing water. Each seat was divided from the next with a single sheet of corrugated iron, with a second sheet forming a makeshift roof. When required, a dock worker could enter a "stall," sit down and relax whilst answering natures call. A copy of the day's newspaper, plus a cigarette, usually made the experience complete.

I made some sort of remark to Harry about them. He smiled, looked at me and said, "Get in early tomorrow and we'll have some fun." Not wishing to annoy Harry or miss the fun, I was in the Gear Shed at 7.30am the following day. Harry was sitting in his usual chair, and on his lap was a fairly sizable cardboard box, filled with small pieces of rope and newspaper that had been rolled into loose balls. It was full to overflowing. Harry looked at me with a big grin on his face and proceeded to spray highly inflammable cigarette lighter fluid into the box.

Harry finished the last drop of his tea, stood up and said, "come with me and do exactly as I say."

Now before I continue, it is necessary for me to explain the characteristics of a 1950's dock worker. To prepare for a long hard day of physical toil, most would start their day in, "The Caff," or local coffee shop/café. A full English breakfast was usually consumed, consisting of eggs, bacon, sausages, black pudding, bubble & squeak, chips and toast. The second place of visit before beginning their workday was, "The Lav." Or London Dock Lavatories By 7.50 am every seat was occupied and Harry was prepared. As we got close to the lavatories, Harry told me to hide behind one of the trucks parked close by. His instructions were very clear. "Watch and do not come out of your hiding place until I come for you." Off went Harry, carrying his cardboard box, and when he got to where the water began to flow under each stall, he set light to the box and gently floated it in the flowing water. Harry quickly ran from the scene as I watched from my safe haven. As the floating fire flowed under each stall, a horrified docker would jump up, usually accompanied by a scream, followed by a string of swear words, then the next poor man would feel the heat and so on, all the way along the seven or eight stalls until the flaming cardboard box flowed into the dock at the far end.

I stood in my hiding place watching this scene, laughing like I never had before. Harry eventually came and got me and as we returned to the Gear Shed, he warned me in no uncertain terms to, "never say a word to anyone ever!" Until I started this chapter of my book, I assure you, I never did!

Chapter 15.

Secondary School, Sex and the Sixties.

It was around the same time that I had my work experience in the docks that I changed schools for the second time.

In those days, us kids were assessed at the end of primary school, to determine what kind of education we would receive in high school. It was called, "The Eleven Plus," The "Eleven" referred to the age at which you were subjected to this, so-called-examination, to determine your future. The second word, "Plus," I have no idea about.

Along with all the other kids in my class, I sat for mine in the spring of 1955.

The system was as follows: those bright and intelligent kids who achieved a certain score earned the distinction of going to High School. Those who did not fare as well, and got a somewhat lower score earned the not so high distinction of going the, somewhat dubiously named, Secondary Modern School.

For us Poplar kid's, this meant George Green High School, for all of those dubbed as, "The smart kid's!

This school was on East India Dock Road, an excellent example of architecture. Dark red bricks, with a large clock, standing proudly from its upper levels. For those who attended, a job in an office, hopefully in the City was both an ambition and a probability.

Secondary Modern, however, was not on any main road. Hay Currie Secondary Modern was built next to the railway. It had none of the grandeur of the High School. The kids who attended there, after, "failing" their eleven plus exam, were dubbed as the dummy's. It was expected that the boys would leave at age 15, and follow their fathers into the docks and become a dock labourer. For the girls, it was try to not get pregnant, leave at 16 then work in Muddies Pien-Mash shop, or next door in Woolworths, in Chrisp Street Market.

NO! This was NOT what happened.

It's true that many of the kids followed this trend, but others broke it and achieved any number of great things.

The point is, that was how, "the establishment of the day," saw it. At the tender age of eleven, us kids were led to believe that this was our future!! Looking back, I find it hard to believe, but it was just the way things were. The good news is, thousands of Cockney kids broke the mould, kicked the trend and led extremely successful lives.

All of this was controlled and conducted by the London County Council, (LCC). They made the rules and determined kid's east end kid's lives, from the lavish building, on the south bank of the Thames, not in East London, but Westminster, opposite the Houses of Parliament, County Hall controlled it all and they were not content with just two high schools! Some bright spark, in their wisdom, came up with the idea of a third high school and it was determined by the, "Hooray Henry's," in the hallowed rooms at County Hall to introduce, "The Secondary Central School."

St Pauls Way Secondary Central was our local school and it was there I began my high school years in September of 1955. I never knew if I was smarter than the kid's at Hay Currie, or dumber than the kid's at George Green, or neither of the above??? Either way, I was to spend the next three, mostly miserable years there.

Class 1C consisted of 32 kid's, approximately 50-50 boys & girls. The school was good, with a great teaching staff. Discipline was mostly maintained by fear & punishment. If any girl screwed up I class, she was sent to Miss Shaller, who would punish by either, detention, which meant staying after class finished, usually for 30 minutes and writing lines of prose, often on the blackboard stating, "I will not screw-up tomorrow," (or something similar!).

The boys were sent to either Mr White or Mr Graceman. Mr White was the sports teacher. He wore white sneakers, or "plimsolls, as we called them in those days. His shoe size was 14, so those plimsolls were huge. Depending on the mood Mr White was in, punishment would be administered with his right plimsoll, at least two whacks on one's backside, or more, as I said, depending on the mood of the day.

Mr Graceman taught Chemistry, and could be found in the "Lab." He was an older gentleman, always wore a three piece suit complete with gold watch & chain. His punishments were more creative.

I remember on one occasion being sent to see him as a result of talking in Miss Lord's class. (This happened quite a lot. I still love a chat to this day!).

Mr Graceman listened to my story, dismissed it as lies, (it most probably was), and took me to his desk where he produced three of his favourite, as he referred to them, "weapons of rebuke." A large wooden spoon, a long flat piece of plywood and a slim bamboo cane were laid before me, followed by Mr Graceman's soft spoken words………………

"Choose one Smith."

Like many kids before me, and many to follow, I made my choice. There was loads of debate among the kid's at Sta Pauls Way as to which "weapon," hurt the least!

I chose the plywood, affectionately referred to by its owner as, "The Whacker."

"Bend over boy," was the command followed by no less than six whacks, all of which stung like I had been bitten by a giant Bee. Once this was over, I was instructed to return, "The Whacker" back to his desk, then get back to class, which I readily and dutifully did. It may be hard to envisage this behaviour today, however it was normal for us kids. It was just the way things were done! As I write my recollections of this event, I am 77 years old and I have never been violent or convicted of any crime, so I leave it to others to determine, did this kind of punishment, used wholesale across schools in those days, help, or hinder my development?

In 1957, during my second year at St Pauls Way, an opportunity presented itself in the form of another examination. While the Eleven Plus determined high school, the Thirteen Plus was available for us kids. It was not mandatory, rather it was devised for those kids who may well have an interest in more practical endeavours, including for the boys, engineering.

My brother had taken and passed this exam and as a result he left St Pauls Way and began attending Poplar Technical College, Secondary Technical School.

This choice was made available to me. All I needed to do was to take the Thirteen Plus, achieve the required pass mark, and follow big brother.

Now to say that I was not an extremely successful academic, would be a gross understatement. At the conclusion of year one in class 1C, I was nowhere near the top of the class! I was not even close. The truth is, I was 31 out of 34 and the only reason I beat numbers 32-34 is because they were absent due to illness for half of the year.

LONDON COUNTY COUNCIL

ST. PAUL'S WAY SECONDARY SCHOOL
BOW, E.3

REPORT FOR *July 1956*   No. in form: 34   Form 1C

Name *David Smith*   Age 12·0 Position:- 31   Average Age 12·0

SUBJECT		Marks obtainable	Mark	REMARKS	
SCRIPTURE				Weak. Should concentrate	MS
ENGLISH	essay	100	53	Fair. Often inattentive	
	Language	100	72	& talkative and distracts	
	Literature	100	54	other children, but cooperative	MM
				in oral work and reads well.	
FOREIGN LANGUAGES—FRENCH		100	34	Disappointing. He must	
				work much harder	MTR
MATHEMATICS		200	72	Very poor.	RJ
GEOMETRY		150	48	Only fair.	MM
HISTORY		100	44	Fair. More concentration	R.
GEOGRAPHY		100	41	Inclined of goodwork but does not	RMG
SCIENCE	Biology	100	52	Fair. try hard enough.	RL
ART		100	48	Fair	JH
WOODWORK		100	39	Tries hard	EFCR
METALWORK					
NEEDLEWORK					
HOUSEWIFERY					
	TOTAL	1200	557		

Conduct *Fair, too talkative and inattentive.* Attendance *354 / 380.*
General Report *The above remarks show that his work has only reached a
fair standard. He is too smug about his own achievements and consequently
will not work hard enough. I am sure he can and will do
much better work.*   M.B. Lad   Master Mistress

............E. D. Smith.............   Parent *G. L. Lathlean* Head Master Mistress
1000 (P & E 22144) 6-54   *Must work harder.*

Dad was not amused………number one son, big brother Bob, was already in his last year at Poplar Tech and was number 1 in his class. Dad was already making plans for me to work in the docks, I was wondering if I should have gone to Hay Currie Secondary Modern School?? There seemed to be no reason for me to take the Thirteen Plus, as it was obvious I would not pass, so in September of 1957, I began my third year of high school education and it was to prove to be a defining year in my young life.

Class 3C, (I think you can see a tend here, 1C, 2C, now 3C?), was no longer 50 – 50 boys & girls. As a result of the Thirteen Plus exodus, there was only 6 of us boys left, with 18 girls completing the class. This is where my problems started.

I was not tall for my age, and I was fairly skinny, certainly not built to be a fighter. The result was something that has happened to kids for years, the awful practice of bullying. I was the weakest of us 6 boys, so it was inevitable that I would get picked upon. I had my head put down the toilet, and flushed. I was pushed around in the playground, in the corridors, etc. If I had any money, that would be stolen from me, and it was only a matter of time until I would be ridiculed by some of the girls. I still have vivid recollections of this, and by Christmas, I was looking for a way to escape. I was considering anything that might get me out of class 3C.

Despite this period of my life held all of this, there was one thing that helped me get through that year and that was, "Sex Education."

Anyone who was at school in East London at that time will tell you that Sex Education was not a part of the school curriculum and they would be correct, however that does not mean that it did not exist! Not in the classroom, with teachers or social workers. No movies to watch, or books to read and certainly no politically correct terminology, especially for body parts.

Sex Education was my lifeline throughout that year, together with the special approval I was given, to sit for the Thirteen Plus in January of 1958, one year later than I should have.

It is often said that at thirteen years old, boys become interested in the opposite sex. For us thirteen year old Cockney boys, this was not true. A better explanation would be to say that we were totally obsessed by girls. They took up at least 80% of our waking thoughts, (plus a great deal more of our dreams)! The good news was that in 3C we were outnumbered by girls 3 : 1. The bad news was that we had absolutely no idea what we were supposed to do with them. Like a dog chasing a car, we were, "hot to trot," we ran fast, we "barked" a lot, BUT, just like the dog, we would be lost if we ever caught up, however this did not stop us, such was the infatuation for girls.

Of the 18 girls in 3C, most were considered to be, "good girls," and therefore not available for Sex Education with us boys. There were however others that had the same infatuation, only for boys in their case and these were the girls we sought out, "to assist in class." All that was now needed was a classroom and that was to be found in a building, opposite the school, on Burgess St.

Bredel House was a block of flats, built and owned by the London County Council. Six stories high, built from bricks & mortar, it is still there today, although now each flat is privately owned.

Whoever the architect was who designed Bredel House, us kids owe him a huge vote of thanks. For some reason, Bredel House had a basement and the door was never locked. Once inside there was a staircase leading down to a very warm, thanks to the boiler and very dark, (and if memory serves, quite smelly), but absolutely perfect classroom for sex.

I managed to endure the days at school, the bullying and teasing etc. because one of the girls in our class, was willing to accompany two or three of us boys, after school to Bredel House basement. It was there our "Sex Education," took place and in case anyone is wondering, it was brilliant! No "birds & bees," stuff for us. No rules, no instructions. Just a warm, dark basement.

Despite my extremely poor academic performance in both 1C & 2C, I had a strong motivator, that being escape from the bullying, so I sat for the Thirteen Plus examination and passed with flying colours. As a result, I began my first year at Poplar Tech in September,1958.

LONDON COUNTY COUNCIL

S

ST. PAUL'S WAY SECONDARY SCHOOL

FORM 3c

REPORT FOR *Year Ending July 1958*

Name **David Smith**   Age 14 YEARS   Average Age 14⅗ YRS

SUBJECT				REMARKS	
SCRIPTURE		3		Has been remarkably lazy	JD
ENGLISH	Composition	61	100	David's work is spoilt by	
	Grammar	37	100	his grammar. He would	
	Literature	60	100	do well with more effort.	
FOREIGN LANGUAGES	French	34	100		
MATHEMATICS		50	100	) Satisfactory, but could be much	GMK
		27	100	) improved if he applied himself more to his work.	
				Improvement	
HISTORY		37	100	Satisfactory. Room for	
GEOGRAPHY		26	100	finds it difficult to concentrate	
SCIENCE		88	100		
ART		54	100	Good	JH
CRAFTS	Woodwork	60	100	Fairly good	E.604
	metal work	75	100		
OTHER SUBJECTS	Tech. Drawing	77	100		
				POSITION IN CLASS ⁴⁄₂₃	
	TOTAL	686	1300		

Conduct V. Good.   Attendance 341/370

General Report David has obtained fairly good results
but might have done better had he made a little
more effort. He is a well mannered boy
who is always willing to help in
the class duties.

W. H. Smith

Parent J. Hancock   Master / Mistress

G. L. Latham Head Master / Mistress

124

By this time, money was starting to play a more important role than it did when we were younger. It quickly became obvious that no money, no fun, so like many kids before me, I got my first job.

A good friend of mine, and one of the, "boys," I hung around with, had got himself a job cleaning cars at Chrisp Street market, every Saturday morning. Now in 1958 not a lot of people in the Eastend had cars, however, the stall holders did, or at least most of them. Graham had a regular clientele and he was earning well. He was very good at cleaning cars, so more & more of the market stall owners wanted him to clean their cars and before long, he had more than he could handle.

I approached Graham, who is still a very good friend all these years later and asked if I could join him. He finally agreed to pass some of his customers on to me, so on the following Sunday morning, I went to Petticoat Lane and purchased a large, chamois leather, bucket and sponge, then on the next Saturday, reported for work.

With some hot water supplied, courtesy of Flo's café in the market, I started cleaning cars. In the summer it was hot work, but in the winter, sometimes with snow on the ground, it was freezing work, but either way it paid well, and I will forever be grateful to Graham for giving me, "a start."

Another way to earn was to get yourself a, "Paper-Round." For me this meant working for Alfie Groves paper shop, which consisted of a wooden shack on the corner of East India Dock Rd & Saltwell Street. This job was all about delivering newspapers to the locals, as quickly as possible! There was little or no other way in those days, long before the internet. The newspapers were huge business, with the printing carried out on huge presses in Fleet street.

There was morning papers, ready and waiting for people to read on their way to work. Afternoon papers, but the papers I delivered were the evening editions.

I was just one of four paper-boys working for Alfie at that time, with each of us having our own, "round," or set area. Mine was the north side of East India Dock Rd, all the way to Stinkhouse Bridge.

There were three evening papers to choose from, The Star, Evening News and The Standard. Alfie's customers had placed their order with him and it was my job to deliver the right paper to the right address, five nights a week. This is how it worked:

Us boys would arrive at Alfie's shop around 4.30pm. We would then, "keep watch," for the paper vans to appear on East India Dock Rd, heading east. Once we spotted one of them we would run to the middle of the road where there was a traffic island, and wait. When the van arrived, a very large bundle of, Evening News, or Star or Standard, depending on which van arrived first would be thrown onto the traffic island. The van "might," slow down, but never stop, so it was our job to hold onto the bundle before it went spinning into the road disrupting traffic. Sometimes the string holding the bundle would burst, and we would have to somehow get all the papers together from between the cars, and get back to the safety of pavement. This was every night come wind, rain or shine!

Alfie would cut the string, and us paper boys would put on our paper bags which were large canvas bags with a strap to go over the shoulder. Alfie would then, "divi-up the papers," for each one of us.

This was repeated three times, (once for each of the different newspapers). Newspapers in those days were counted, and delivered in, "Quires." A quire was 25 newspapers, with every 26th one stacked, "off-centre," to leave approximately 1 inch sticking out. When the bundle was cut, Alfie would give each of us the correct amount of quire and we would jump on our pushbike's and start our rounds. Mine was the largest of the rounds, so when I peddled across East India Dock road to start, I was carrying five and a half quire of newspapers. Depending on how many pages were in each copy, 142 newspapers adds up to a lot of weight, especially for a fourteen year old boy on a pushbike, however that was the job and I was lucky to get it. As Alfie would often remark, "if you don't like it, there are plenty of other boys ready to replace you!"

Sunday morning was about delivering the Sunday papers, all before 8.00am, then we would go to every house on our round to collect the money for the pares to be delivered in the coming week. For this, I received the grand sum of 15 shillings per week, or AUD$1.50 per week in today's money.

While delivering newspapers in February of 1959, I actually lived the words in Don McLean's song, "American Pie."

Don McLean is an American singer/songwriter, who at the age of thirteen was a "Paper Boy," in his hometown of New Rochelle, New York. While folding newspaper in preparation for his, "paper route," he was shocked, along with the rest of the world to read about Buddy Holly's death in Iowa. Some years later when he wrote the song that became a huge hit worldwide, he included the words, "bad news on the doorstep," which referred directly to the newspaper headlines telling of Holly's death in a plane crash.

At the very same time, in Poplar, East London, I was performing thee same task, literally delivering, "bad news on the doorstep." My interest in Pop songs was just getting started and the new age of, "Rock-n-Roll was well upon us. One of the Boys, Sam lived in Kenworthy Rd, Homerton. As a kid he had gone to his local church, St Mary of Eaton, which was just around the corner from his council flat home. That same year, the Reverend John Oates, saw the strong need for a youth club. Fourteen years had passed since the war ended and massive progress had been made in rebuilding London, but for the thousands of us kids, there was very little to keep us out of trouble. Sadly many went to gaol for criminal activity.

Recognising this the "Fifty Nine Club," opened its doors in the Eaton Mission, a building adjoining the church.

Although I was underage at the time, (not yet sixteen), along with Sam I went along on April 2, 1959 for the grand opening. Cliff Richard, (now Sir Cliff Richard), sang his, newly released recording, "Living Doll."

The next day I took my best pair of trousers to a tailor repair shop in Willis St, and paid the man to alter the bottoms from twenty inches, to fourteen inches, or "Drainpipe pants, "as they were known. The next week at the 59 club, I felt very cool. The old man was not impressed, but as I paid for the alterations myself, (from my paper round and car cleaning jobs), he let it go. I was now officially a youth, just in time for the, "Swinging Sixtie's."

My three years at Poplar Tech were fairly uneventful. Being an "boys only school," my Sex Education days," were over, (but the memories still linger!), and discipline was stronger than St Pauls Way, courtesy of the headmaster, Mr Philip Ian Partridge, or PIP as he was affectionately known.

PIP was the third of three great teachers I encountered in my East London schooling. Mr Enever, at Susan Lawrence was the first, followed by the headmistress at St Pauls Way, Miss Lathleen. Unbeknown to me, Miss Lathleen had been aware of the bullying I endured in class 3C. On my las t day at her school, she sent for me to go to her office. Until I arrived there I had no idea as to why.

Miss Lathleen was a woman in her mid to late fifties. To run a school in East London in those days, she needed to be strong, and indeed she was! A rather large woman, always well-dressed who spoke with a quiet, yet firm way, was sitting behind her large wooden desk when I entered her office. She began by congratulating me on passing the Thirteen Plus and asked me how I felt about going to Poplar Tech? I stammered out some sort of answer before she told me about the bullying. She told me she was well aware of what had happened in 3C, (she never mentioned if she knew about the basement in Bredel House!), and asked me if I was changing schools, to, "run away from the problem?" Without waiting for an answer, she continued to advise me that bullies are everywhere, not just in her school. There would be bully's in Poplar Tech. bully's when I leave school, etc. She told me that bullies were cowards. They were usually all bluff and needed others to, "back-them-up!" She told me that I cannot run away forever. I must make a stand, and I must do so as soon as I start my time at Poplar Tech. I remember her words until this day, but as I left her office, I wondered, how do I do this? How do I, "out-bluff," the bullies'? I was to find out on day one of term one, in the form of two boys, both bigger than me. I cannot use names, other than to say that one of these had an Italian sounding name, and the other went on to play County cricket. They had a plan to throw me out of the classroom window, (as they had already done with some other kids). Miss Lathleen's words were in my head, and I knew I had to somehow, "call their bluff." The problem was, they weren't bluffing. The moment of reckoning was upon me. If I failed now, life would become miserable again. There was only one thing to do. "BLUFF!" Time to bring in the big guns in the form of big brother Bob. He had just begun his first year as a tertiary student, studying for an Ordinary National Diploma in marine engineering. The building was immediately adjacent to the secondary school so I knew I could use this to avoid my upcoming fate!

"You throw me out the window you will pay dearly. I will get you for it and if I can't, my brother is next door and he will, so back-off!" The two bullies looked at each other and I could see they were pondering what I had said. Was it a bluff? Did he actually have big brother there? Would he come after them?

At that point another skinny first year walked past. The bullies decided he would be easier than me, so I escaped and poor old Ken W. was bundled up and dumped out of the window. I was left alone and was never bullied again, thanks to the good advice from Miss Lathleen and a big bluff, (and big brother), from me.

Mr Partridge, PIP was the third great teacher. An unusual man who looked distinctly out-of-place in the slums of East London. He was a very tall man, but very thin in build. The adjectives, "skinny & lanky," were often used, but despite this, his appearance was always immaculate. Starting from the ground up, Pip's shoes always sported a very high shine. The crease in his trousers was razor sharp, and part of a three-piece-suit he always wore. I never saw him without his suit jacket, open at the front to reveal his waistcoat, bottom button open, gold chain crossing from pocket to pocket and his gold watch sitting there, ready to be lifted out, the dial exposed, followed by him announcing the time. In the top pocket of his jacket was a handkerchief that matched his tie. The cuffs of his white shirt, (he never wore any other colour) showed about one inch below his jacket sleeve. The only word to accurately describe PIP's appearance was Immaculate. He would walk the corridors of Poplar Tech and he knew every one of the 350 or so pupils by name. He was also the man who was responsible for keeping order and administering punishment. If you were sent to PIP by your class teacher, you were in big trouble. I tried my best to avoid this, however in late 1960, I failed.

After acting the clown in English class, I was sent to see PIP. There was no escape! A school with that many Cockney boys in it, needed a firm hand, and PIP had one. He always smiled. He always spoke in a very friendly manner. Even when he told you to bend over, for six of the best, he was as calm as could be. I was certainly not calm as I knew what was coming.

PIP would bend the can as he walked around in his office, all the time, I was bent over, arse-in-the-air, waiting. He was a very religious man, so as he administered the punishment, he would quote from the bible, or his favourite hymn. On this day, each swing of the cane was accompanied by Psalm 23, with extra emphasis from PIP on the passage, "I will fear no evil for my rod & staff comfort me." Six whacks later and a big smile from PIP and I was back in class. Three days later my arse was still sore.

I was one of many pupils at Poplar tec that went through the same ritualised punishment back then, however for those of us still alive today, PIP was a great man, fantastic teacher and played a huge part in getting all of us ready for the upcoming adult world. RIP. PIP.

Chapter 16.

Smog & Jehovah Witnesses.

At the end of May, 1961, I finished my schooling at Poplar tech and armed with my two GCE's O-Level, (General Certificate of Education, Ordinary Level), walked out onto Poplar High Street for the last time.

I was totally unaware at that time, but I had been given an excellent education at Poplar Tech. So where would I go next?

Some of my classmates had followed in my brother's footsteps, joining a shipping line as a cadet and returning to Poplar Tech for their studies, prior to going to sea in the merchant navy. Others went into the docks, following their family tradition.

At that time, my father, three uncles and three cousins were all dock workers, so it would have been really easy for me to follow suit, but for some unknown reason, I did not want to. This decision, together with the next one I made were to shape my future in a way that I could never have imagined.

On August 14, 1961, I reported to the offices of J.G. Sneath, Electrical Contractor's, in Solebay Street, Stepney Green, London E1. It was my first day as an, Apprentice Wireman, Journeyman & Electrician. I had applied in July and once accepted, I signed indenture papers that bound me to the company until I reached the age of 21. The two other new boys and I stood in front of a large wooden counter, known as, The Stores," with some of the older apprentices, waiting our instructions as to where we go and which electrician we would be assigned to. As we waited, the managing director of the firm came in. Each of us apprentices stood to one side, and as he passed, with said a polite, "good morning Sir," and touched our hand to our forehead. We were watched by the two supervisors from behind the counter and if we failed to acknowledge and address the boss in this manner, we would be on report. That's the way things were done back in the day!

My first job was to go to Towler & Sons Riverbank Works in Bow. A very large shed was under construction and Sneath's were installing all of the electricals, including lights, power, overhead crane, etc.

I rode my pushbike through Mile End, Bow, and over Bow Bridge, and once there reported to Ron Bryson, an excellent electrician and a good man to learn my new trade with.

Towler's was the first of many locations I worked in that by today's standards would be considered as, "Seriously Hazardous!" I had purchased a Boiler Sit to wear on-site. This was the entire extent of my protective wear. In those days, helmets, steel-toe-cap-boots, were not mandatory. We worked on the steelwork, 40 feet above the ground with no safety rails or harness. That was the way it was! At lunchtime, we sat on a box, outside of the electrical room, As we were eating and drinking, one of the, "Cladders," the team erecting the outside walls of the shed, was cutting sheets of asbestos, with a circular saw. Ron & I were oblivious to the dangers. We know better now of course. I spent my time as an apprentice working in different factories, offices, shops etc, some of which were just as hazardous as the asbestos clad shed at Towler's.

One such factory was alongside the river lee, almost under Bow Bridge. I no longer remember the name, but I clearly recall working there in the summer of 1962. This particular factory processed and produced carbon black. I have absolutely no idea what is was used for, (pencils perhaps?), but the air inside was full of a fine mist. Along with the electrician I worked with, we installed lights in the roof. At the end of each working day, we were told to shower in their change rooms, prior to leaving for home. This suited me well as we had not hot water or shower in Ellesmere Street, and a shower was absolute luxury. On the Friday night following a week in the factory, I put on a white shirt, best suit and headed off to the Two Puddings pub in Stratford. After a couple of hours of dancing in the upstairs dance hall, and failing to, "Pull," (failed to meet a girl and take her home), I went home, and straight to bed. The next day I looked at my white shirt and it had a large black ring under each arm and the collar was also jet black. It seems I had absorbed all of this at the factory, and it came out as sweat.

Another location was in Millwall, on the Isle of Dogs. A large factory with the name, "Associated Lead Manufacturing," proudly displayed above the entrance. I spent more than four weeks there, only to find out years later that the premature death toll for employee's was greater than 100 times that of the population.

Hubbard's Paints also had a factory in East London. I was sent there to work for an older electrician, by the name of Bert. He was ex-army, stood bold upright and always had a self-rolled cigarette in his mouth.

As we walked down a flight of stairs on the factory floor, Bert was explaining what the job was. Without warning, a very large lady, with paint on her hands, face and clothing, ran out from between the stacks of paint and grabbed Bert around the neck, putting a very strong, "choke-hold," on him. I can still see his face, neck locked under her large arm, his face beginning to turn bright red, and the cigarette still firmly held between his lips.

I stood there not knowing what to do, when another lady walked up and spoke the attacker. "It's OK Mary, just let the nice man go please," were the words she said, and instantly Bert was released. Fortunately he was unharmed, and the second lady who had come to Bert's rescue explained to both of us that Mary had worked at Hubbard's for many years, and like many of their employees, had been mentally affected by the lead that was used in the paint manufacturing process. Both Bert & I were very wary after this incident and we witnessed a great deal more of unusual behaviour from other employee's, all due to the amount of lead they had been exposed to.

Around the same timeframe, again whilst working with Bert, I was sent to an old hospital, opened in 1934 north of the town of Wickford in the county of Essex, Runwell Mental Hospital. On arrival we were told that there were more than 200 patients in the hospital and we were not to engage or speak with any of them. The staff were dressed in white and the, "inmates," were in normal street clothes. It was a very scary place for an eighteen year old Cockney boy. Years later I saw the film, "One flew over the cuckoo's nest," and it reminded me of my time at Runwell.

One particular incident happened on a cold afternoon. It was raining and us apprentices were outside one of the buildings, standing in a ditch, hauling huge, heavy cables that would supply the building with electricity. As we worked there, soaking wet and covered in mud, a window above us opened, and a patient's head appeared. "What you doing?" he said. We all looked at each other and remembering the instructions, we did not answer him. "Looks like hard work to me," he said. Again, no replies from us. "You should join me," he said, "I'm in here by choice, I'm not crazy!" He went on, "I commit myself here every month or so. I can leave anytime, but why would I? It is nice and warm in here plus I get three good meals a day. Most of the female patients are in here for sexual obsession problem, so I have a great sex life. I go to the movies most weekends, have a pint in the local pub, then return here. I love it!"

One of the other apprentices looked at the rest of us, freezing cold, up to our knees in mud and said, "And we think he is the crazy one?"

Travelling around to all of these various factories and locations was usually on my pushbike. I had sold the 24 inch wheel black bike that Dad built for me and bought myself a full size bike, bright red in colour, and the best part was the Sturmey Archer, three speed hub gear in the back wheel. It was second-hand of course, but as far as I was concerned, it was, "really cool."

Another job I was sent on was, "William Warnes Rubber Company." Built on the side of the River Roding, the factory had been there for close to 100 years.

I would leave home around 7.00am, make my way towards the West India Dock Gate, cross over the River Lee on the Iron Bridge and into Canning Town. Passing Rathbone Street Market on my right and staying on Barking Rd until the junction of Beckton Rd. Onto the A13 and keep going until the bridge over the river. The big new shed being built stood out from the A13 and it was here I worked for about six weeks.

Sneath's had a, "gang," working on this site. About a dozen or so, tradesman and apprentices. I was the youngest apprentice, so the job of, "teaboy," fell to me.

This meant going all over the construction site to find each & every Sneath employee on-site, to get their, "morning tea orders." These orders would be for, bacon-sandwiches, egg sandwiches, bacon rolls, toast & dripping, etc. Each order would be different, some wanting HP Sauce, some wanting tomato sauce, some with none. I would write each and every one down, alongside each individual's name. It was clearly understood that failure to deliver each order, exactly as requested would be met with abuse and possible violence, I.E. a clip across the ear!

After collecting the money to pay for all of the orders, I would go to the change hut and collect the two very large enamel tea urns, place one on each handlebar of my bike, then head off to the local, "Caff," (café to you non Cockney's).

I would wait patiently outside the Caff, until my orders were ready, then with one tea urn, full of hot tea on each handlebar of my bike and a canvass bag full of hot rolls and sandwiches, I would ride back to the site, where all the crew would be waiting in the hut.

Each paper bag had the person's name on, and I would pass them out, after which I would pour the tea into everyone's tea mug. This was repeated again at lunchtime and again at 3.00pm, six days a week.

Practical jokes were all part of growing up and working in East London in those days. I could tell hundreds of these; however one comes to mind that happened in that hut at William Warnes Rubber!

It was my second week on this job, that Sneath's head office sent a new foreman to oversee all of us. Now this was noy unusual in itself as these things happened quite often as different foreman were sent to certain jobs. The difference this time is that this new foreman was new to the firm. Nobody knew anything about him. It turned out that he was not a nice man, or as one of the boys put it, "he's an arsehole," and indeed he was. His style was authoritarian and his behaviour was to bully, especially us apprentices. Now as I said earlier, at morning teatime, al the mugs were on the bench, ready to be filled. The new foreman had a very large white, with a blue rim enamel mug and painted on the outside were the words, "Bills Mug. Touch and you die." This was typical of the nasty arrogant man he was, so it was decided that he would he needed to be taught a lesson.

Just before morning tea the following morning, one of the boys sneaked into the shed, found the foreman's mug, drilled a hole in the bottom, then screwed it to the bench. Morning teatime came and all the boys were inside, eating and drinking tea, when in came Bill. Hr grabbed his sandwich from the bench, than putting his right hand index finger into the handle of his mug, he tried to lift it. The screw held fast and Bill's index finger left its socket, accompanied by a screaming yell of pain from Bill. The upshot of all of this is that he had to go to hospital to get his dislocated finger fixed. That afternoon we had a visit from one of the supervisors from head office, then after talking to the men, left. The following day, Bill was transferred to another job, complete with his very sore finger. The mug stayed fixed to the bench as a reminder!!

Of the many different places I worked during my apprenticeship, the sugar refinery at Silvertown sticks in my memory. There were two factories in Silvertown, both of which belonged to the same company.

Tate & Lyles two factories were both built on the north bank of the River Thames, less than a mile from each other.

I would ride my bike from Poplar, over the iron bridge which crossed the river lea, then turn right onto Silvertown Way. This rad eventually went to North Woolwich and the famous Woolwich Ferry, however I did not travel that far.

The first of the two buildings could be found on the right hand side of Silvertown Way, with the railway running in front of it. The large white stone building was, "Lyle's" built on that site by Abram Lyle, and opened in 1883 by a Scotsman from Greenock, who produced a thick sweet product, originally known as, "Goldie," but was more widely known as, "Golden Syrup," which was widely used and loved by us lids.

The second factory, also found on the right side of the road and also with railway tracks in front, was, "Tates." Opened in 1868 by Henry Tate. This was where I spent 18 scary weeks in 1952.

Both of these factories were on the riverbank and both relied on ships bringing in sugar cane from various places around the world with the majority coming from The West Indies.

The refining process produced many things, including Rum, but the main product from, "Tateses," as we referred to it, was sugar. Brown sugar, white sugar, demerara sugar, sugar lumps etc, they made them all.

I worked in most of the different buildings there during my time, but the main building was where they packed all the different sugars for distribution. It was here that I had the biggest scare of my life.

To understand how & why this happened, it is necessary to appreciate the size and complexity of this huge factory complex. Despite being in the middle of London's Docklands, with the huge Victoria & Albert Docks next to it, a popular target for the Nazi Luftwaffe in WWII, Tateses never stopped production. In fact Tateses factory produced sugar from its inception in 1868, through both world wars, and still continues to do so. In 2018 Tate's celebrated 140 years of sugar production at its Silvertown Refinery. At its peak production, Tateses employed more than 5,000 staff. The packing floor was almost exclusively women.

Located on the first floor of the main building, the main packing floor consisted of production lines, conveyor belts running at speed, with the staff, all dressed in white, their hair tied up inside a white scarf, all complemented by white gloves, sitting alongside each line, boxing & bagging each product as it came passed.

So what could be scary about this? The stories that surrounded this place were many & varied, however it seems that these ordinary Cockney Girls had more than a regular sense of humour. It seems they would pounce upon any foolish male, (especially any young foolish male), that might enter their domain, and if the rumours were true, that poor unfortunate guy would be waylaid, manhandled and would eventually be allowed to leave the packing floor, minus his trousers and underpants. Needless to say that as an 18 year old male, I spent my time at Tateses, terrified of what might happen if I was sent to work there. Thank goodness this never happened.

Many years later, a book was written with the title, "The Sugar Girls," Tales of Hardship, Love and Happiness in Tate & Lyles Eastend."

Some simple facts about Tate & Lyle. Henry Tate and Abram Lyle had factories less than one mile apart, yet never met in person and hated each other. It was not until they were both gone, their respective sons' merged the two companies together. Henry Tate was an avid collector of art and upon his death bequeathed the majority of his collection to the British Nation, in what was to be known as, "The Tate Gallery, " now The Tate Modern.

In those days, my working week consisted of 45 hours, made up by 8.00am to 5.00pm Monday to Friday and 8.00am to 1.00pm on Saturday. One evening in December of 1962, I finished work at the scheduled time and prepared to ride my bike home from Silvertown to Poplar, just as I had done for the recent weeks, however, this day was very different.

Smog, a nasty mixture of fog and smoke was a phenomenon that Londoners had grown to understand all too well. In 1952, "Great Smog of London," forced the Government of the day to consider new, "Anti-pollution legislation," and in 1956 they passed the "Clean Air Act," which restricted the burning of domestic fuels in urban areas, producing, "smokeless zones."

London was black from the years of smoke. Buildings mad from white stone were black. It is estimated that after the end of WWII until the 1956, in excess of 5,000 people died as a result of smog.

It was December 4, 1962 that will forever be in my memory. I had ridden my bike to Tateses that morning. It was a particularly cold, damp day and the fog was thick before I left home at 7.00am. Daylight hours are short at that time of year, but on this day, there were none. It did not get light as we knew it. The sun just never pushed through. Midday was still cold and an eerie fog hung over the Thames. By the time 5.00pm came around, darkness had descended, and the fog became smog.

I prepared to ride the familiar roads home, but the smell in the air filled my nostrils. I later learned that the Sulphur Dioxide in the air was seven times higher than the safety number. It made breathing very difficult, plus my eyes began to sting. As I went out of the factory gate and turned left onto Factory Rd, I took my scarf from around my neck and placed it over my nose and mouth, tying it as tight as possible behind my head. Despite having gloves on, my hands were freezing.

I pushed my bike across the railway lines, then I turned on my front and back lights, mounted the saddle and began the ride home.

Visibility was almost impossible. Even knowing the roads as well as I did, I was nervous. Fortunately the route home was very simple. Follow Silvertown Way to the intersection at Barking Road. Turn left at the traffic lights, over the iron bridge, pass Poplar Hospital, turn right at Chrisp Street then home.

Just as I was about to start my journey, I heard a loud voice calling out from behind me. I strained my eyes to see where this came from, and through the smog, I saw the headlights of what I took to be a lorry. I heard the door open and out of the darkness, the face of the driver appeared. He explained that he needed to get to Stratford and that from his seat in the cab, he could not see anything. His visibility was down to a few feet. He could however see the red light that I was on the back of my bike. His request was simple, that was to follow my red light along Silvertown Way, until we reached the intersection at Barking Road, after which he would attempt the remainder of his journey without me.

He kept the window of his lorry open in order to communicate with me, and within minutes I set off. Every few minutes the driver would yell some reassuring words, letting me know that he was still following the red light. My visibility was about 6 feet, and I kept my eyes clearly on the kerb, and rode my bike as slowly as possible.

The smog lasted the entire time I was riding with the lorry following me, until eventually the traffic lights at the intersection appeared out of the blackness.

I took my bike and placed it against the wall of the building that I knew to be the Imperial Palace, a picture theatre we went to a skids, and quickly returned to the extremely grateful lorry driver. He asked me for one more favour before we parted company, that was for me to wait for the traffic light to go green, then walk across Barking Road in front of his lorry. He was very nervous, so I agreed.

Once we were in the middle of the intersection and it was safe to do so, I yelled for him to proceed, and wished him a safe journey home. It was at that time I realised that I had assisted more than that solitary lorry driver. The little red light on the back of my bike had led a procession of vehicles safely along Silvertown Way. As I returned to retrieve my bike, Lorries, cars and buses were crossing the intersection. I stood there for ages, watching all of these vehicles and felt quite proud of my little part in helping them all through the smog.

That day was the first of 6 days that the smog lasted, causing many people to stay home. Even getting to work was close to impossible, and only emergency workers etc were required to do so. This leads me to something that happened, somewhere around this time, that beggars belief.

My Fathers best friend was a fellow Tally Clerk, working for the same company, J. Leete & Sons. Both men were casual tally clerks and relied upon their skill & wits to get enough work to put food on the table. His name was Alan Howard and he lived in a small terraced house, running off of West Ferry Rd on the Isle of Dogs. Married with two children, he rented next door to his mother-in-law, (of whom he told many a funny story), however it is what happened to him in December of 1962 that I will relate to you.

It seems that the thick, black, nasty smog kept most people at home, however, it did not deter the Jehovah's Witness people, from knocking on people's doors to sell their particular brand of religion.

Alan related this account of that day himself, and I will attempt to do justice to it here.

Sometime in the morning of that week, Alan's wife answered a knock on her front door, to find five people. They identified themselves as Jehovah's Witness' and began their message, handed her copies of their magazine and asked all manner of questions about her and her religion. Despite her best polite attempts to get them to leave, she found herself floundering, however when one of the group suggested they return that evening and conduct prayers for her and her family, she reluctantly agreed, and managed to close the door, no doubt very relieved.

When Alan arrived home later that day, she had to inform him of what she had done and agreed too. She was very nervous, believing he would be upset with her, however, she underestimated her husband, (and she was not the only person to make this mistake, as I will explain in a later chapter). He was not at all upset, in fact he said he would look forward to it! To say his wife was confused at this, would be a massive understatement. He asked her what time the Jehovah's Witness" were due to return, and learning it was to be at 6.o'clock, he instructed her to organise dinner early, then once everything was put away, she was to take the kids and go next door to her mother and stay there until he came for her. This she did!

Alan's house was very similar to the one I grew up in. Terraced with two rooms up and two rooms down. The difference was that in Alan's house, the front door led directly into the small lounge room. With two armchairs, a table and four chairs in the room, there was very little space for anything else, but like all of those cottages, there was a coal fireplace, which as soon as his wife was next door, Alan proceeded to pile high with coal.

By the time 6.o'clock arrived, the temperature outside would have been around freezing point.

When the knock on the door came, Alan opened the door, and welcomed the five Jehovah's Witness' inside, closing the door as quickly as possible behind them.

They shuffled into this small room, and tried to find enough room to stand together, hoping to tell their stories and spread their word. All five were appropriately dressed for the cold English winter weather, with heavy overcoat's, gloves, scarves etc.

Alan made his way back to his armchair, sat down and looked at the five. He said nothing!

By now the coal on the fire had done its job and the temperature in the room was heading north. A small room with six people and a large fire gets very hot, very quickly. The group began their well-rehearsed ritual, and Alan sat back in his chair and listened. At every opportunity, Alan would ask a, "meaningful question." As time passed, the heat began to get to the group of five. Coats were undone, scarves and gloves removed, however they still stood, preaching their religion, as slowly the sweat began to appear on their foreheads. One of them asked Alan if he could take his coat off, to which Alan replied, "No! Please continue with your sermon."

Alan kept those five Jehovah's Witness' in his lounge room for a total of two hours, at which point they were desperate to leave. Eventually he stopped asking questions, thanked them politely for coming, and opened the front door. As they went out into the freezing cold night air, Alan thanked them yet again, and advised them they were always welcome to return. They never did!

Chapter 17.

Mods, Lambretta's & Dance Halls.

I was a teenager when the sixties' hit London, just 15 years of age, with no idea how fortunate I was to be in that city at that particular time in history.

I have heard it said that "if you remember the sixties'. you most likely weren't there?" Well I certainly remember the sixties', and I was definitely right there when they hit.

Barely fifteen years after the end of the devastation inflicted on London by one of the largest aerial bombardment on any city in history. Beginning on September 7, 1940, London and in particular the docks situated in the east, were systematically bombed by the German Luftwaffe continuously for 57 days & nights.

"The Blitz," as it was so named, (From the German word, "Blitzkrieg,") or "lightning war," continued with mainly night bombing until May 11, 1941, more than 8 months in total. More than 40,000 civilians died, another 100,000 plus injured and in excess of 1,000,000 homes damaged or destroyed.

As the fifties rolled away and the sixties began, the rubble and destruction of those awful eight months had been cleared away. My world of Poplar and East London looked like a patchwork of old buildings, huge empty areas of land where once buildings had stood, and of course, building sites. Pubs were open and people were smiling and enjoying life again. Pearly Kings & Queens appeared on the streets, men played games of darts in the pubs and many a party could be found on a Saturday night. A Crate of beer, a piano, a bunch of Cockney's and a, "good old knees-up," was heard again. Standing around a piano in someone's house, (a lot of people had pianos in their homes in those days), singing "maybe it's because I'm a Londoner," or "knees up muvver (mother) brown," or even doing the "hokey-cokey," the room full of cigarette smoke was what is was all about, at least for the "Oldie's!" Us kids had other ideas.

Back in the fifty's, music was very much bland and boring, with the majority of it coming from the US. Perry Como singing, "Magic Moments," Doris Day's "Que Serra Serra," etc. but towards the end of that decade, things started to hot up. Bill Haley & the Comets, "Rock Around the Clock," caused people to get up from their seats in the cinema and dance in the aisles. The Waltz, the Quickstep and other ballroom dancing styles gave way to, "The Jive." The sixties came and with it, "The British Invasion," as the Americans called it.

From Liverpool came, "The Mersey Beat," The Beatles, Gerry & the Pacemakers, The Swinging Blue Jeans, just to mention a few whose music would change the entertainment industry forever. In London, The Rolling Stones, Dave Clark Five, The Tremeloes, Cliff Richard, Joe Brown & the Bruvvers, the list goes on. It was new, exciting and is still seen as a revolution in music today.

Dance Halls everywhere were suddenly the place to be and could be found everywhere. The Streatham Locarno, south of the river, The Lyceum in Central London, The Tottenham Royal, on the northside The Hammersmith Palais in the west, where The Rolling Stones began their career and my all-time-favourite The Ilford Palais in the east.

The majority of the Dance Halls were owned and managed by an English company, Mecca Dancing Ltd and they had very strict rules. At the Ilford Palais, entry meant, "appropriately dressed." This meant no jeans, no boots, no leather jackets, which is one of the reasons the phenomenon of, "Mods & Rockers," came about.

By the early sixties, the 59 Club had transformed into a Motorcycle Club by the then motorbike-riding Vicar, Reverend Bill Shergold. Denim Jeans, leather jackets and boots were the uniform for anyone who rode a motorbike, known in the day as, "Rockers." Entry to, "The Palais," was not possible.

When one of the boys got himself a Lambretta, it was obvious where we were going next. Mods! It made all the sense in the world to us Cockney lads. When two of the boys followed, only this time buying themselves Vespa's, I knew I wanted the same, so some time in the early sixties', (I'm not sure exactly when), I sold the old trusty pushbike and bought myself a second-hand red & white Lambretta Li 150.

One of the boys was not actually an east ender as he lived in the City of London. His family owned and ran a Pub, namely, "The Primrose," in Bishopsgate. It was there that we would all meet, every Tuesday night. It was a scene to be beheld, typical of the sixties', Vespa's, Lambretta's all lined up outside the pub. Every one of them adorned with spotlights, chrome mirrors, everything and anything that showed the world, "We are Mods!"

Weekends were eagerly anticipated. Friday night was, "The Two Pudding's," (or, "The Two Pudden's as we called it), a great pub in Stratford.

Saturday was almost always, "The Ilford Palais," a Mecca owned ballroom on the high street. Every Saturday night at The Palais, we followed the same ritual. First was to be appropriately dressed for the night out. This meant highly polished, "winkle-picker-shoes," with Cuban heels. Two piece suit, (just like The Beatles wore), white shirt, plus the mandatory slim-jim tie. The dress rule for all the Mecca Dance Halls was posted outside. If you did not comply you did not get in!

Once inside, was a sight to behold. Girls-Girls-Girls and more Girls, all dolled up in colourful dresses, high heel shoes and "big hair." We were in heaven!!!!!!!

There was always a group, playing the best rock-music, followed by Phil Tate and his Orchestra, accompanied by a guest singer. The last dance of the night was always played by his band, always a slow romantic tune with the lights turned down low, stars appeared in the roof of the Palais. It was known as, "Dreamtime." It also meant that this was every guy's last chance to, "Pull," (get himself a Girl), or make his way home afterwards without one. I must admit, this was often the case for me. The consolation prize was to grab all your mates who had failed, head for Brick Lane for Curry! A very poor substitute, but it was the best outcome.

On one particular Saturday night, I travelled with a good mate of mine, Brian in his car. It was to become a very special night………………………..for Brian that is, unfortunately not so for me!

To understand and appreciate what transpired on this night, you need to understand a little on how things were done on those days. It was the, "Age of Jive." The days of the Quickstep, Foxtrot & Waltz were long gone. Bill Haley & the Comets changed all of that when they recorded, "Rock around the Clock in 1955.

In the Palais, Jive was all the rage. If a guy wanted to dance with a girl, he could walk up to her as she stood on the side of the dance floor and simply ask. This method however was just not our style. The, "norm," in those days was for the girls to go onto the floor and with one of them taking the man's role, they would jive together. If any of us boys wanted to dance with them, we would follow the accepted practice of, "splitting them up!" This meant walking out onto the dance floor, and asking if we could dance with them.

On this particular night, there were not two, but three girls, jiving away on the dance floor. Brian was the first to suggest that we, "split them up." The third person was Sam, another school friend.

Before we could walk across the dance floor, (they were on the opposite side to us), we had to decide, "who gets who?"

The criteria for this was not what you may think. Not good-looks, not clothes or shoes, not dancing abilities. The main criteria was a lot simpler than all of these. It was height! Brian was the shortest, around 5ft 5 inches. Sam was around two inches taller than him, followed by me at 6 feet. As we looked at the three girls swirling and spinning, I very much fancied my chances with the shortest of them. Brian quickly shut me down on this, explaining that if I took that one, and Sam took the next one, he would have to dance with the third girl, who appeared to be very close to 6 foot tall herself. I reluctantly agreed to, "take the tall one," and we set off across the dance floor, hoping that we would not get rejected, (as would often happen, making the boys look like total idiots, walking off the dance floor alone).

On this occasion, we, "got a result," meaning we were not rejected. Brian danced with the shortest of the three girls whose name was Sheila. They dated after this, married the following year, and were together for more than 50 years before Brian passed away in 2018.

Sam danced with the second girl, (I forget her name), but she refused to let him take her home.

I danced with Viv. She was not that tall, in fact she was 5 feet 8, but the three inch high heels took her close to my height. We jived away for a couple of dances, then that magic time arrived……………….Dreamtime. This was the big test. If Viv did not want me to take her home, she would not stay with me for this last dance. Good news is that she did stay, so once the dance was over, we both got our topcoats from the cloakroom, (it was wintertime and very cold), and headed outside to get the bus to Seven Kings, the suburb in which she lived.

We walked the six or so blocks from the bus stop at Seven Kings station to where Viv lived. She was a nice girl and we got along well. On reaching her home, we went through the awkward ritual of, "do I, or don't I try to kiss her goodnight?" I am a gentleman, so I refuse to elaborate what may or may not have taken place, however once the goodnights were said, it was time for me to return to Poplar and home for the night.

I retraced my steps back toward Seven Kings, delighted that I had, "pulled that night," and walked over to the bus stop, only to find that I had missed the last bus heading west. I entered the train station hoping to get a train, but unfortunately, no trains.

I did not know it at that time, Seven Kings Station to Ellesmere St Poplar is a distance of 7 miles. With insufficient funds for a taxi, the decision was already made. A cold brisk 7 mile walk was the only way. To "Cut a long story short," as they say, two and a half hours later, sporting very sore feet, I climbed into my bed exhausted, (but still very happy that I had pulled).

In case you are wondering, I did see Viv again. It was at Brian & Sheila's wedding and, "no," she was not there with me.

The Ilford Palais was a regular haunt for us lads, together with the Tottenham Royal and the Lyceum. It was a great time to be a teenager and a great place to live. In case you are in any doubt, I loved growing up in the Eastend and even after 50 plus years in Australia, I am still a very proud Cockney.

Chapter 18.

Bunce, The Old Bailey & Cockney Pride.

My days as a "Mod," were really quite short-lived. I had been to Brighton a few times and had a great time, but one wet, cold & rainy morning, my adventures as a Mod on a Lambretta came to a swift end.

At the time I was working in a factory that produced aluminium foil, on what was then known as the, "Thatched House Roundabout," a rather large public house on what was then the A13 road. Just before the roundabout there was a long slow rising bridge that took the traffic over the railway line, before dropping back down at the roundabout. The road was black tarmac, soaking wet from the rain, and for a Lambretta with very small wheels, a serious traffic hazard. As I begun the rise toward the top of the bridge, a very large rubbish truck, originally heading west, was now heading northwest, wheels locked and tyres slipping and sliding was headed in my direction. With traffic in front and behind me I had nowhere to go!

I am not sure what exactly happened, but I clearly remember separating from the scooter, watching it disappear under the rubbish truck, while at the same time I was in a sitting position, legs outstretched in front of me, hands on the road to steady me, continuing across the bridge, until coming to an abrupt stop on the other side of the bridge.

I looked around to see the car that was following me stop, (how he did this I will never know) and my beautiful Lambretta Li150 jammed tight under the still-moving truck. The result of all of this was threefold. The first being that the Lambretta was completely destroyed. Its days of transporting anyone around were sadly over.

The second was I could not afford another Lambretta.

The third, (and most influencing factor) was Mum absolutely forbid me to buy another, "Italian Death-trap."

Decision made!

By this time I had passed my driving test, and purchased my very first car, a shiny black 1954 Austin Somerset. It was to serve me well for quite a few years.

A car was a much more sensible choice for an apprentice electrician. It was my job to carry my tradesman's tools from job to job, plus we often came upon an opportunity to, "make a few extra quid." Many of the places we worked entailed removing old and damaged wiring from the buildings and replacing it with new. This led to large amounts of old wire and although it did not belong to us, (legally speaking), it was always considered as, "Bunce," our word for scrap copper that when taken to the local scrap merchant, would be converted into cash, often significantly large amounts of cash. I freely confess that my 1954 Austin made numerous trips to the scrapper, carrying copper in the boot on the outward journey and "cash for the boys, "on the return. We considered Bunce as ours and ours alone. It was not stealing. It was considered as essential in cleaning up the environment.

Sometime around 1964, my brother Bob was working, as a contractor in a large factory in Wembley, North London. As part of the job they were doing, a large amount of, "Bunce," became available. As was the usual situation, it "disappeared," from the factory, but on this occasion things were very different. When the management of the factory discovered their coper was no longer on the premises, they did something that nobody suspected.   They called the Police!

Back in those days, this was unheard of. It was a well-known and accepted custom that whoever pulled the scrap copper out, kept it and sold it as their own. It was Bunce! Surely everyone knew that?

Within a few days, brother Bob received a summons in the mail, to appear at Court, (I think it was The Old Bailey, but could well be mistaken), on a date set for three weeks later. Our family had never encountered anything like this before. We lived in a house with no hot water service, no bathroom and an outside toilet. We did not have money for lawyers, but we did need to save Bob from a possible prison sentence and criminal record.

The problem was………..HOW?

The charges against Bob stated that on the day that the scrap copper was stolen, the gatekeeper at the factory in point, gave a statement to the Police that he had witnessed two men, who he identified as two of Bob's fellow contractor's, carry the copper across the factory yard and put it into the boot of Bob's car. He went on to say that he then saw Bob drive the car away.

The factory management put a value on the scrap copper of £570=, a large sum of money in the mid-sixties.

The old man, Bob & myself sat at the old table in Ellesmere St. This was serious. Bob could go to prison. After a short time, Dad decided what to do. As we were unable to get any legal representation, we had to do the next best thing. Ask the smartest person we knew to help!

The following day, Dad returned home from work and told us he had spoken to his mate and he had agreed to help. That evening there was a knock on the door. It was no other than Dad's friend from work, Alan Howard, the same Alan Howard that had dispatched several sweaty hot Jehovah's Witness' form his home some 12 months previous.

Gathering around the table once more, Alan was bought up-to-speed on the charges. After a few questions, Alan sat back, scratched his head, then gave us his strategy.

He explained it like this: If Bob did not drive to work on the day in question, then the copper could not have been loaded into the boot, therefore Bob could not have driven away, proving Bob was innocent. In order to make this strategy work, Alan would appear as a witness for the defence. In his evidence he would say that on the day in question, he drove to Ellesmere St to pick up Dad and take him to their workplace. He would state that Bob had already left the house when he arrived, and his car was parked where it always was, in the street, outside of 46 Ellesmere

St. The plan had been hatched, everyone knew what to do & say. Alan returned home and we waited for the Court date to arrive.

I had never seen the inside of a British Court but in 1964, the Court I was sitting in was a forbidding site. Heavy dark wood panelling all around the walls, (most likely very old English Oak), small windows allowing very little light inside, a unique, "musty smell," people in black gowns and white wigs.

I sat in the public gallery watching all of the events unfolding in front of me. Bob, along with two other men I did not recognise, were in the dock, the judge sat looking down on the proceedings, the men in their wigs sat in the middle. The charges were read out aloud by the Clerk of the Court. All three accused said they were not guilty.

A man was then bought into the Court and placed on the witness stand. The prosecuting lawyer asked him to state who he was and he replied he was the gatekeeper at the factory. He went on to tell the Court that on the day of the theft, he saw two of the accused carry the copper across the factory yard and place it into the boot of a car. He then stated that he witnessed Bob driving the same car away from the factory.

The lawyer for the defence, (I assume a Court appointed one as we had not hired anyone), did not cross examine the gatekeeper. Not a good start for Bob!

There were no other witness' for the prosecution, so the next person to be called was Alan, the first & only witness for the defence.

Alan followed the script, as he said he would, telling the Court about seeing Bob's car in Ellesmere St on the morning in question. The defence lawyer thanked him and handed over to the prosecution. As he stood to question Alan, he straightened his wig, smoothed down his gown and began asking questions.

"How can you be certain that it was in fact, the same day as the theft?" he asked, to which Alan replied, explaining that it was also his wife's birthday, so he could not have mistaken the date. The next question was about the car. "How can you be sure it was the accused's car you saw, and not one of a similar make & colour?" Alan's reply was simple. "Bob's car is a two-tone-blue Ford Cortina, GT," which is quite rare and also happens to be one of my favourite cars."

At this point it was obvious that the prosecuting lawyer was starting to get frustrated with Alan. He decided to take another approach. "Did you drive to Court today Mr Howard, or did you travel by public transport?" Alan replied. "I drove to Mile End, parked my car in a side-street and come to Court on the London Underground from Mile End Station."

In rapid-fire the next question was put to Alan. "Did you park behind another vehicle at Mile End this morning?" Reply from Alan was affirmative, then the prosecutor quickly followed with another question, "Please tell the Court the make and colour of the vehicle that was immediately in front of your vehicle this morning, when you parked in the side-street in Mile End!" Alan's reply shocked me, as it must have shocked Dad, Bob and everyone else in that Courtroom. "I am unable to do that sir," was Alan's response.

Now at this stage, it was obvious that our learned friend, the Prosecuting Lawyer was sensing blood! The expression on his face changed from one of possible frustration, to someone who could smell success. He looked very smug as he immediately continued his questioning. "Mr Howard, can you explain to this Court how you can so accurately remember details of a vehicle you claim to have seen more than three months ago, and yet cannot tell us the make or colour of a vehicle you parked behind, less than three hours ago?

Alan stood on the witness stand. The "Poker-face-expression" on his face never changed. The prosecutor waited for this casually employed, poorly educated, semi-illiterate Cockney Eastender to answer. The pompous and arrogant look on his face told what was happening in his head. He had this eastend lout on the ropes, so to speak and he knew it.

Alan spoke quietly but clearly, answering the question in full. "The car I parked behind in Mile End this morning was completely covered by a large tarpaulin sheet. It was therefore impossible for me to tell this Court the make or colour."

The next few seconds brought absolute silence to the Court room. The expression on the prosecution lawyers face changed from smug to deflated. The judge could not stop himself from smiling. He then asked if there were any more witnesses to be heard and on hearing there were none, he ruled that the three accused men were innocent of the charge.

The well-educated and experienced learned lawyer had assumed that a Cockney accent meant that its owner was less than capable. He was wrong and he lost. I wonder if he learned from the experience?

To this day I have no idea if Bob and his mates did in fact steal the copper, believing it to be Bunce. It is of no consequence. The judge found him not guilty and that is all that matters.

What happened to both Bob & Alan in that Courtroom was far from an individual event. Cockneys have been judged, (or should I say mis-judged) for their unique accent and colourful expressions for many many years.

At about the same time that this farce played out in the Courtroom, I saw an advertisement in the newspaper for Customer Engineers. The company advertising was IBM. In those days they were one of the largest suppliers of office equipment in the world. The "Golf ball Typewriter," was unique and was filling typing pools and offices all over the world, including the UK. The advertisement was for people to be trained on these machines for the purposes of repairing and maintaining them in the customers offices.

I read the advertisement carefully and as far as was possible to judge, I had all the necessary qualifications and skills required. After replying to the ad. I received a letter to attend the IBM offices, which at that time were located on the A4 in Hammersmith, West London for an interview.

I was delighted at this. If successful it meant a possible career with a very large and respected company. Computers were in their infancy so I would have an opportunity to get into this exciting industry from the beginning.

On the day of the interview, I put on my best suit, white shirt and "sensible "tie. I made sure I arrived early. This was important.

My first task was to take some tests, IQ and mechanical aptitude. I passed these with flying colours. The next step was the interview. I was shown into a large office, and declining the offer of tea or coffee, it began.

After approximately 20 minutes or so, the gentleman interviewing me stopped the interview and told me he was not going to hire me, but would explain why. He said I would have no problem with the training, and would be very competent to repair and service their products. He then explained that the majority of their customers were legal firms and the like, with many of them in the City. He would be uncomfortable sending someone into that environment who had such a strong Cockney accent. He went on to say that as I was still very young, (I was twenty at the time), I should take elocution lessons that would help me to, "speak better," and re-apply again in the future.

He then terminated the interview and I made the return journey from west to east London.

Over the next few weeks, I thought about what he had said, I also thought about Alan Howard and his role in Court. I decided that I was an Eastender. A Cockney boy, born &

bred. The man from IBM's advice was totally, "out of order." I saw it as an instruction for me to become something or somebody that I am not. For me to become an IBM employee, I was being asked to change who I was. I decided it would not happen and it never did! After more than 50 years in Australia, People I meet will say to me, "what part on the Eastend do you come from?" I love it! Many years after this event, my Cockney accent came into question. I was living in Hong Kong at the time when the lease held on Hong Kong by the British was coming to an end and after 99 years, the Territory was to return to the control of China. There were numerous celebrations being held, and as I worked for a large Australian Corporation, I was invited to many of them.

One particular event was a dinner, held in The Presidents Room on the top floor of the Hong Kong Stock Exchange. It was part of the US Embassy.

The pictures adorning the walls of the room were all of past American presidents. Lincoln, Grant, Roosevelt etc. I was one of eight guests, and we were waited upon by no less than 11 waiters, who served 12 courses. I think you get the picture?

I sat next a Scandinavian gentlemen, who like me had grey hair and an accent. He was a Vice President of the International Monetary Fund.

During the course of dinner, questions were being asked about each person's position and background. I quickly realised that all the other attendee's that night had

University Degree's, Masters of something or other with one of them being a Doctor.

Sometime during the course of the evening, my Scandinavian neighbour turned to me and said, "what about you David? What is your background?"

My reply began with the words, "Very much different to all of you good people, however, here it is." I told them about the bombed sites for playgrounds, Ellesmere Street with no bathroom, Tate & Lyles Sugar factory, etc etc etc. I told them about emigrating to Australia. I even told them about having a market stall in Petticoat Lane.

When I finished this summarised, rendition of my life, my Scandinavian neighbour turned to me, shook my hand and said, "what a great and full life you have lead. I wish my story was half as interesting as yours."

There was never any need to change anything, especially because other people requested it.

I may not have attended Oxford, Cambridge or any other famous tertiary establishment. Instead, I attended the University of Life and graduated from the East London School of Hard Knocks. Those qualifications have served me, (and no doubt thousands of other boys & girls over the years) very well.

Oh, and in case you are wondering, despite not following the advice of the man in IBM, I did in fact work for IBM in Australia for eighteen years, rising to the rank of junior executive. More about this, if & when I write a second book, which I intend to creatively title, "A Cockney Kangaroo 2."

Chapter 19

"Cabbage down the Lane."

As 1965 approached, the dreaded, "Slum Clearance Act," demolishing the old buildings, damaged by the blitz, finally caught up with us Smith's in Ellesmere Street. To be perfectly honest, it was not before time, in fact it was well overdue. The sign on the outside of number 46 read, "Arthur Cottages, Built 1864." In the 101st year of their life, we moved out and the bulldozers moved in.

The way things were done is as follows. The London County Council, (LCC), would offer the families being evicted under the Act, three choices. Each choice was given individually, so if the first was not accepted, the second offer was made. Once an offer was accepted, the LCC would pay for the removal of that family to the new home. The downside was that, if all three offers were rejected, the LCC would have the power to evict, and in many cases they did exactly that.

Despite our old rented house being what it was, I did not want to leave. Even the thought of a bigger house, with hot water and a bathroom, plus inside toilet was not enough. I loved 46 Ellesmere Street. It was my Eastend home and I was being told to leave it behind! Not my idea of a, "good-time!"

Mum had no intention of going to live in one of the Tower Blocks that were springing up around us. She made that point very clear to dad and the LCC. She had lived in various houses all of her life, and she would live the remainder of it in the same way. She wanted a house.

The first offer was a house, a three bedroom house with all the things listed above. Mum & dad went to see it, and rejected it. It was in a Council-built-estate, completed in 1958 and unfortunately in 1965 it had a bad reputation as a, "high crime place full of bored troublesome teenagers!" Irrespective of whether this reputation was true or false, Mum rejected offer number one.

The second was a small house, somewhere in Eltham. I never saw it, but for some reason, Mum did not like it, so rejection number two transpired.

With only one more offer available, we were getting quite concerned. The LCC must have felt the same way because they sent a man around to talk to Mum. After this discussion, we waited to see what would happen, and within three days, offer number three arrived in the post. It was a three bedroomed, two story house in the south-east London suburb of Bellingham. It was in a quiet square, terraced, with a short alleyway between the houses, leading to a back garden. It even had an Appletree there.

To everyone's relief, Mum accepted this one and 126 Playgreen Way, Bellingham S.E.6 became our new home. It was about this time that I began dating a young lady who lived in Basildon, Essex. I was working a rotating shift at the newly built, (in fact it was still under construction in 1965), Greenwich District Hospital, on the corner of Woolwich Rd & Vanbrugh Hill .

I would travel the 30 miles or so to Basildon and stay overnight. Her family were also East Londoners, Hackney and Clapton Pond. They had made the move to the then new town of Basildon where they had both started new businesses. Her Mum had a car hire and panel repair shop and Dad, a Clothing manufacturing business. It was this second one that gave me the opportunity to enter, "The Rag Trade," and become a genuine, "Cockney Barra-Boy." Let me explain!

The clothing busines her Dad owned was in the business of producing hundreds of ladies dresses, various colours, designs and sizes. He produced for two customers, the first being Marks & Spencers Retail Stores and the other was the largest Mail-Order company in the UK at that time, Littlewoods Catalogue.

I was intrigued by the hustle & bustle of this, "factory," with all the girls on their sewing machines, working at a frantic pace, yet still managing to have a chat to each other.

The dresses were cut, stitched finished, inspected, then packed ready to go off for sale in a M&S shop or by mail from Littlewoods. As I watched on I noticed a clothes rack, three quarters full of various designs and colours, all similar to the ones being made at the time. I asked what they were there for and the answer was, "That's the Cabbage Rail."

It seems that the process being followed was that his customers would supply and order for a fixed amount of dresses, in assorted sizes and supply the material for the production run.

I went on to learn that a good cutter could lay-up the material supplied in such a manner, that they would produce more than the required amount of dresses required by the order. All of the "spare dresses," were known in the rag trade as Cabbage.

I looked closer at the Cabbage Rail and the dresses were excellent. Various styles, colours and sizes, but all exactly the same as the ones being delivered to the two customers. This led me to ask the question, "what happens with all the Cabbage?"

The answer was simple. Just like brother Bob, myself and others in the construction business saw scrap copper as Bunce, Cabbage was the equivalent in the rag trade. It was sold to anyone who wanted to buy it, cash only and no questions asked.

Let me say that I was no Lord Sugar, however I could see an opportunity for a young Cockney Electrician, so I made him a cash offer right there and then, and became the owner of approximately 75 dresses, straight from the Cabbage Rail.

It was now time to make a decision! How does a 21 year old go about selling dresses to ladies? After all, I was no milliner, or anything like one! When I asked the old man, (Dad), his advice was very useful! From memory he said, "how the bloody hell would I know."

Taking this excellent advice on-board, I gave it some more thought, then the answer came to me.

Petticoat Lane.

It was simple really. I worked all weekdays on rotating shifts, 6-2, 2-10 and !0-6, but I did not work on Sundays, so Petticoat lane Sunday morning Market was the way to go. I drove to Middlesex Street, Spitalfields, still in East London, found the office for the Sunday Markets, then after paying the princely sum of 5 shillings to the man, I became the proud owner of a, "site," in an alleyway that stretched between Middlesex Street & Goulston Street that transformed every Sunday morning to become Petticoat Lane.

Next stop was to a small used car lot, in Whitehorse Rd, Limehouse, to buy myself a proper vehicle in which to transport my goods. There I bought myself the ideal mode of transport, a 1960 model, grey-green Bedford Dormobile. It not only fitted all of my stock into the back, it had racks on which to hang my, "cabbage," upon. I, was officially in business for myself.

The next Sunday I was out of bed and into the Dormobile before 6.00am, driving from Bellingham, across Tower Bridge, then joining all the other stall-holders, I set up my stall for the first of many times, on my rented site in Petticoat Lane.

It was a cold, but dry morning that particular day, and I set up my dress racks, one each side of my site, and one across the back, taking good care to make sure the dresses were in size order, the size 10's to the left, then 12's, 14's etc, all the way up to two dresses, size 26!

By 8.30 am, the crowds began to arrive and my stall was very popular with the ladies. They were both smart & savvy and knew exactly what they were looking at.

Marks & Spencer's dresses and Littlewoods catalogue dresses that they knew were selling for £7.10 shillings right there in front of them for only £3.00 each.

At this point I need to explain something. Because the dresses I had purchased were "cabbage," they had no labels sewn into them. No Littlewoods or M&S, but the ladies didn't care in the least. They came to the market to get a bargain and these dresses were definitely that.

The only labels to be found were cardboard labels, held on with a string loop, with the size printed upon it.

Each prospective customer would rummage through the rail to find their size. Now I was very naïve at the beginning of my career as a barra-boy, but I quickly learned something about how ladies shop for clothes.

Size is King!

They would hold the dress they admired up in front of them, (no changing rooms in Petticoat Lane Market), then ask their friend if it would fit? It didn't take me long to realise, that if a lady could fit into a dress that was one size smaller than she would normally wear, it was as good as sold.

In no time at all, I became one of the best, "guessers of ladies sizes," in the market. Let me explain:

Step 1. Quickly run my eye over the ladies as they walked towards my stall. "Guess," their size.

Step 2. Make sure all the labels showing the size of the dress were easy to remove.

Step 3. Keep some spare labels handy.

Step 4. If the lady looking at the dress was, "guessed ," as being, say a size 14, take the label off of a size 14 dress and replace it with a size 12.

Step 5. When the lady said, "I will never fit into a size 12," tell her to bring it back next week for a replacement or money back.

I sold practically all of my 75 dresses on that first Sunday and not one of them was returned the following week.

Needless to say, I was a very successful, "entrepreneur barra-boy."

I had my stall in Petticoat Lane for almost two years, but the romance with the lady in Basildon came to an end, and sadly, so did my days as a barra-boy.

Chapter 20.

A new wife and a new life.

I first saw Staff Nurse Joan Gallagher on Nelson Ward, one of the old multi-bed wards on what was left of St Alfeges Hospital.

My foreman in the electricians shop was a well-dressed, very polite man by the name of Bob Warren. He was much older than me, (48 is very old when you are aged 24) but he told me all about this beautiful nurse and insisted I go with him to meet her. As we approached the entrance to Nelson Ward I saw her, standing by a patients bed, in her crisp brand-new blue Staff Nurse uniform. Bob had not exaggerated one bit.......she was indeed very pretty, with incredible red hair, cut into a, "bob-style." I can see her still today, more than 50 years later. That vision will stay with me until I leave this world.

Joan Gallagher, (right hand side), in her Student Nurse's Uniform, 1965.

Now seeing Joan at this time posed a problem for both of us, the reasons being that she was engaged to be married to a young Irishman from Limerick and I was in the same arrangement with the young lady from Basildon. These arrangements remained in-place, until, that is Easter Friday, 1969.

For reasons I no longer remember, the Basildon romance ended sometime in March of that year. Easter Friday was April 4, and someone in the hospital where both Joan & I worked, told me there was going to be a party, hosted by the student doctors at the sister hospital, The Miller Hospital in nearby Deptford.

Now there were hundreds of nurses in the two hospitals, so when I was invited to this party, I may well have thought about how lucky I might be on the night, but I did not think that way at all. My first thoughts were to wonder if Staff Nurse Joan Gallagher would be there. That vision of her on the ward was still firmly in my head, and I was secretly hoping she might attend?

The party began at around 8.00pm, and I arrived soon after. It was a typical students party, a big room, lots of people, plastic glasses with a huge big stainless steel hospital bowl on a table, into which every kind of alcohol had been poured, (including some clear liquid being added by a student, from a medicine bottle?). The music was very loud, people dancing, others standing around talking.

After a couple of drinks from the, "punch bowl," I plucked up the courage to ask a girl to dance. She too had partaken of the booze and we got on really well.

She told me her name was Donnelley. She was not a nurse, but her sister was. She lived in Plumsted with her sister and her sisters best friend, and the three of them had come to the party together. Her sisters friend was none other than Joan Gallagher.

A few minutes later I saw Joan and when she saw me, she gave me a smile. I asked her to dance and as we shuffled around on the floor, I told her I was no longer engaged. She looked at me and said, "same here………… my engagement ended two weeks ago."

Needless to say, we spent the rest of the time at the party together, after which I took her home.

Joan and the two Donnelley sisters lived in an old house in Maxie Road, Plumsted. Just like my old home in Ellesmere Street, it too was designated to be demolished under the Slum Clearance Act, but in the meantime, the Landlord was making a few quid, renting it to the three girls.

I saw a great deal of Joan over the next couple of weeks. We got on really well and the relationship developed quickly.

When I told Dad about the budding romance, he was delighted. He worked with Irishmen in the docks, Patrick Dempsey, George Farrell, Connie Murphy, to name a few, in fact he loved everything Irish. His favourite film of all time was, "The Quiet Man," with John Wayne and the beautiful redhead actress from Dublin, Maureen O'Hara. Joan was, "a keeper," as far as Dad was concerned.

Mum, however had been raised a Catholic and attended a Catholic school as a young girl. The story goes that she came home from school one day, looking very sorry for herself and hiding her hands from her mother. When her mother did eventually see her hands, they were extremely swollen, with heavy red welts across the palms. When asked what happened, she was told that one of the nuns had used the cane on her. The reason for this was because she was unable to recite the Catechism. Mum was kept home from school the next day, and in fact never returned to a catholic school. Adelaide Daisy Hayes, (nee Beck), went to the school instead and upon finding the nun who had hurt her eldest daughter, proceeded to give her a full-on punch on the nose, telling her that if she heard of her hurting anymore children, she would return to do the same again.

Now this experience could well have left my mum having a dislike of Catholics and of course, Joan is very much a practising catholic. This was not the case. My mum was a lovely and kind person. Joan was accepted, no questions asked.

Three weeks after the Miller hospital party, Joan & I were moving into a serious relationship. If we were to continue seeing each other, we needed to sort out some ground rules.

The first one was the difference in our religions. In 1969 that was a big thing and the cause of many failed relationships.

The second was my long-held ambition to emigrate to Australia. Clearly there was no point in developing our relationship further if we would end up on opposite side of the world. I decided to address the second issue with Joan, my logic being that if the emigration issue was not resolved, the religious one would disappear.

On a Sunday evening, sometime in May of 69, as Joan & I were sitting in the little front room in Maxie rd., I decided to tell her of my plans. It had never been mentioned before, so I told her I had always wanted to go to Australia to live and I believed she needed to know this before we got further involved. After I had made this statement, I sat back and waited. It went very quiet.

Joan just looked at me and I was unable to decide if she was shocked, happy, sad? I had no clue!

After what felt like a lifetime, (all of 5 seconds in reality), Joan reached over to a shelf that was beside the fireplace. She picked up an envelope and passed it to me. She had a huge smile on her face.

When I looked at the envelope, it had the Australian Coat of Arms on it and the address, Australia House, London. Joan had decided months before, that she too would emigrate to Australia. The envelope contained her application for assisted passage.

As they say in the movies, "the rest is history." Less than 11 weeks after meeting at that party, on Joan's 23rd birthday, we became engaged. I am afraid I have to admit, my proposal was hardly worthy of a, "romantic one," in fact it was very poor. Let me explain.

When my parents got engaged, the old man did it, "eastend style." So did I!

On June 19, Joan's birthday we took a drive from Plumsted to Deptford. After parking the car, (and leaving Joan sitting in it,) I walked to the shops, and went to the same shops dad had gone to years before. The name escapes me now, but it was on the high street and had three brass balls hanging out the front. You guessed it; the shop was a pawn shop. I went in, picked out the ring I wanted and paid in cash. Good Cockney logic dictated that, as the price of second-hand jewellery was tax exempt, I would get a better ring for the same money, so what could be wrong with that? I took the ring back to Joan, handed her the ring box and said, "try that on." I started the car and began the drive back to Plumsted. Joan had a look of surprise, (maybe even a little shocked), however, she put the ring on her third finger, left hand and had a huge smile on her face. Needless to say, she has, "reminded me," about this, "proposal," on more than a few occasions!

Four weeks after that we drove to Fishguard in South Wales, boarded the ferry to Rosslare, then made the short drive to Wexford, Joan's hometown in Ireland.

Joan was the youngest of four girls, the second youngest, Rita was married and had just moved to New York. The next was Florrie, who at the time was a young widow with four children. Florrie was an extremely talented seamstress so on our second day in Ireland, I drove Joan, Florrie and her eldest son John the 75 miles to Dublin, where wedding dress material was purchased. By 7.00pm on that same day, armed only with the material and a photograph taken from a magazine in London, Florrie produced a beautiful, (although very short), exact copy of the London magazine wedding dress.

It was on this trip I was introduced to the mother-in-law, Ita Gallagher and father-in-law John. It was 1969. I was English. I was NOT a Catholic, all of which were a huge potential problem in Ireland in those days. Where would we get married? Church or Chapel as they would say? Will Joan be, "allowed to practice her religion?" What about any children in the future. What religion will they be? What school will they attend?

All of this, before any questions about my political beliefs regarding Ireland's independence and the, "Troubles," in Belfast. How will this union work?

Fortunately my, soon to be in-laws were delightful, open-minded people and I am happy to report that not one of those, "potential problems," ever eventuated. They were very supportive and agreed to come to the wedding in the future.

Less than six months after our first date, on October 4, 1969, Joan & I were married at St Patricks Catholic Church in Plumsted, South East London.

A few weeks prior to this, Joan had applied for a flat, one owned by Greenwich District Hospital. Lister House was one of three buildings, half-way up Vanbrugh Hill in Restell Close. They were specifically for Hospital staff and as Joan was a Staff Nurse and I was employed as an electrician, we qualified. Flat 16 on the fourth floor of Lister House became our first home together. It was fully furnished, which suited us, because we were about to submit our application to Australia House for assisted passage. It was to remain our home until we emigrated the following year.

The campaign by the Australian Federal Government to encourage people to emigrate to Australia was in full swing in 1970. It had been running for a number of years and was responsible for thousands of families leaving their native countries, Greece, Italy, Yugoslavia, Hungary, Ukraine, etc. History shows it to be a very successful campaign, with second and third generation's all started by those, "New Australians," of which Joan and I were about to join.

Shortly after submitting our forms to Australia House, we were called in for an interview. The reason for this interview was to determine if we would be eligible for the, 'assistance scheme," and would we be of sufficiently good character to meet the criteria? I found this most amusing, given that the first, "New Australians," were thieves, murderers, cut-throats, rapist and all things bad, sent to Australia, or as referred to in English newspapers of the day, "The Colonies," and here we were being assessed by their dependants(??) as to our character? Ironic or not?

We had both been Police checked, cleared as crime free and therefore eligible for the £10 scheme. With my qualifications as an indentured electrician, plus Joan's as a registered nurse, we were, "passed as acceptable."

The next step was a medical, plus a chest x-ray and by January of 1970, we were officially given permission to emigrate, using the, "assisted passage scheme." This meant we paid £10 and they paid the balance. This also meant that if we failed to stay in Australia for a minimum term of two years, we would have to pay the government back, on a pro-rata basis, all the money they paid towards our fares.

We were given the option as to when we wanted to depart and we were also given the choice of ship or aeroplane. This second option was introduced in the latter part of the scheme and was the one we chose.

We continued to live in Lister House and work in the hospital, all the while saving up as much money as we could before August 10, 1970, the day determined to be the day we left our world behind, in search of a new one!

Chapter 21

Twenty cents please, Essendon airport and the, "Wig-Wags!"

Our Scottish aeroplane, chartered to Qantas, with its cargo of English migrants, or "Pommies," as we were to be known in Aus., left Gatwick at around 9.00pm. The first stop was Bahrain. I had no idea where in the world Bahrain was, but we landed there. It was dark as we left the plane, and were herded into a tin shed. There were steel tables and chairs for us to sit at, together with some cold drinks and water. It was very hot, very humid and the air-conditioned comfort of the plane was very welcome, once we re-boarded.

The next leg of our flight was to Kuala Lumpur. Again I confess, I had absolutely no idea where that place was either. More fuel for the aircraft, more water for the passengers, and we were off again, this time on our final stage of the journey to Sydney, Australia.

It was sometime around 6.00am when we landed in Sydney. It had been 26 degrees Celsius at Gatwick on our departure, somewhere between bloody-hot and stinking-hot in Bahrain & Kuala Lumpur, then we arrived in Australia, "the land of sunshine & Oranges," it was pissing down rain and 5 degrees Celsius……………had we been conned?????

Leaving our faithful old, "tartan-clad-interior," Caledonian Airlines plane on the tarmac, we entered the Kingston-Smith Airport. Our journey had taken around 30 hours, but for £10, it was a bargain.

We were about as far away from Poplar, Greenwich and Wexford as it was possible to be. Any further and we would round the earth and begin towards home again. We were met by Australian Federal Government Staff, who checked us into our new Country, then showed us where to go for the next, (and final) leg of our big trip. For us this was Melbourne in the State of Victoria, a mere one hour flight, due south from Sydney, however, to join that flight, Joan & I had to travel from the International Terminal at Kingsford-Smith Airport, to the Domestic and this entailed a bus ride. Joining a group of Pom's from our Gatwick flight, we boarded a bus, sat close to the back and waited for the driver to arrive. Within minutes, this poor man arrived, looked at his passengers, sighed and began to walk down the aisle of his bus, talking to each row of people as he did so. I refer to him as, "this poor man," because I could not but wonder why he would willingly take a job that entailed driving, "whinging bloody poms," across the airport, at 6.30 am on a cold Sydney winters morning?

He made his way down the centre of the bus, until he approached Joan & I, sitting quietly, extremely tired and very keen to get to Melbourne.

"Tickets!" he said, not looking at anyone in particular.

"Tickets," he again exclaimed, this time with more gusto and looking straight at me. "I have my airline ticket." I replied. "Does this look like a bloody aeroplane?" he said, voice even louder than before.

"Bus Ticket" he repeated for the third time. "Sorry," I said quite meekly, "I don't have one."

"Twenty Cents," he said, holding his hand out. You see, when we boarded the plane in Gatwick, we were told, there had been some sort of mix-up with the bookings. We were not on the register, however, there was to be two seats on the aircraft, and they were ours, which in fact, there was, thus we flew halfway around the world.

Getting across the airport, however, was not included. Everybody else on the bus had tickets except Joan & I.

"Twenty Cents," came out of the poor bus drivers mouth again and it was blatantly obvious that without his getting twenty cents from Joan & I, we were staying where we were, IE Sydney Kingston-Smith-International-Terminal.

As luck would have it, I had changed some English pounds into Australian dollars & cents at the airport, so I promptly handed over forty cents and in return received two tickets, then within minutes, we were on our way to the domestic terminal to join our Ansett Airlines flight to Melbourne's Essendon Airport.

Every time somebody refers to me as a, "ten-pound-pom," I correct them and say, "ten pounds and twenty cents in my case." I'm a stickler for getting the facts right!

The idea of getting UK people to emigrate permanently to Australis, was the brainchild of the Chifley Government in 1945. It officially ended in 1981, however the peak years were in the 1960's. More than one million people took advantage of the scheme, and a large majority of those spent their first days, weeks, months, and in many cases, years in the numerous migrant camps spread around the country.

When our plane touched down at Essendon Airport, at approximately 10.50am on August 12, 1970, we were met by friends, John & Jean Saunders. John, (always referred to as, "Sam"), had been a friend of mine since our days at Poplar Tech. He had married Jean in 1969, and they had migrated shortly after. As we walked across the tarmac. We could see both of them, standing and waving from the term9nal roof to welcome us. Once inside the terminal, we were met, not only by these two friends, but also Rosco & Spider, who we had known in London, and a whole bunch of their friends. We were made to feel extremely welcome in our new country, and it was the nicest feeling having all of these, "new friends" there to greet us.

Sam & Jean took us out to their car and we began our last part of our journey to Mentone, a beach side suburb of

Melbourne, however on the way, it was time for lunch and our first ever visit to a real Aussie Pub.

I am unsure of where, exactly the pub was, somewhere in East Melbourne maybe? Sam parked the car and we walked into the pub; in exactly the same way we would have back in England. This was a big mistake. As soon as we entered, the barman looked up, and we heard the words, "No ladies in the bar." This took us "poms," by surprise. What did he mean? Are ladies banned from pubs in Australia?

In the 1970's, the rules for ladies in pubs changed, but in August 1970, the rules of, "Men only in the front bar," still existed. We were unaware of course, but the barman quickly explained that ladies were very welcome, however only in the lounge, which was next door. We had mistakenly gone in through the wrong door and we never made that mistake again.

Following being, "thrown out of the bar," but then enjoying a great lunch in the lounge, it was time to go to our first new home in our new country.

58 Warrigal Rd, Mentone is a large block of land, on which stood, (and still does today) a large wooden colonial style house, typical of the area. Painted in a pale cream colour, with a corrugated iron roof, also painted but this time in green, it stood majestic, complete with a white picket fence, dominating the corner of Warrigal Rd and Como Parade East.

There were two smaller buildings behind this lovely house, one of which was a one bedroom cottage consisting of a small lounge room, even smaller bedroom and a, "two way bathroom," which we were to share with the tenant in the other cottage.

As we made our way through the garden and into our new home, we were greeted by more, "new friends," all of whom were a part of Spider & Rosco's mates. Geoff & Leanne, John & Elaine, although complete strangers to Joan & I had brought bread, milk, cheese etc for us. There was a huge bunch of flowers sitting in a vase on the small dining table. We were very fortunate to have such lovely people to welcome us to Australia and are forever grateful to them all. We sat around and talked for a while until the jet-lag and the tiredness kicked in. Joan & I had been travelling for a total of 42 hours, two hours in a mini-cab to Gatwick, 30 hours in a Boeing aircraft with tartan seats, a twenty cent bus ride in Sydney, a one hour Ansett Airlines flight to Essendon and finally a car ride to Mentone. After a quick shower in our shared bathroom, we fell into bed, very happy and totally exhausted.

It was light outside when we awoke. August 13, 1970 was to be our first full day in Australia. As we sat drinking our morning coffee, we were excited, but also a little apprehensive, (more truthfully pretty much scared!).

We knew where we were, but where exactly where were we? As we discussed this, we went to the door, to be greeted with frost on the grass outside. It was a clear but cold day in Mentone, then without warning, we heard a noise that was both strange and unexplained. By now we were at the front gate, and a worker from the laundry that was next door to 58, was standing smoking a cigarette. He must have noticed the look of bewilderment on our faces. He took a few steps closer and said, "have you never heard the wig-wags before?" With this, he pointed across Como Parade East and it was then we realised, for the first time since arriving, that the railway ran parallel to Como Parade and there was a, "level crossing," complete with barriers, to stop cars and pedestrians from crossing Warrigal Rd. As the barriers came down, and the red lights began to flash, very loud bells, with their distinct notes began to ring out as additional warning of the approaching train. "Ding-ding-ding-ding-ding," affectionately known to all the locals as, you guessed it, "the wig-wags."

We stood outside number 58, the worker returned inside the laundry and Joan & I looked at each other without saying a word. We knew we were thinking the same thing. Which way shall we walk? Where are the shops? Are we close to the beach?

We had no car, so we walked across the railway line, made the decision to turn right on Como Parade West to see where it would lead us. I remember holding Joan's hand and telling her that we should stay on this road, so we would not get lost and would be able to, "follow the railway line to find our way back home."

This was the beginning of our new life in Australia. What adventures lay ahead? Would we like it here? Would we stay? Where would we work? What kind of car would we buy? Would we have children? More questions than answers as we set off on our first walk.

For 26 years I had lived in London, a true east ender. A true cockney.

I was about to become, "A Cockney Kangaroo."

The End.

Printed in Great Britain
by Amazon